DUMB CROOKS
HALL of SHAME

ALLAN ZULLO

Scholastic Inc.

To my youngest grandchildren,
Jack Manausa and Ella and Dash Gorospe,
who are guilty of stealing my heart.
—A.Z.

Copyright © 2018 by The Wordsellers, Inc.

ISBN 978-1-338-22264-7

10 9 8 7 6 5 4 3 2   18 19 20 21 22/0

Printed in the U.S.A.   40
First printing 2018

Book design by Charice Silverman

CONTENTS

DUMBEST OF THE DUMB

Our prisons and jails are crammed with hardened felons, chronic crooks, and bad-choice troublemakers. Some of these miscreants are the most inept lawbreakers this side of the straight and narrow. These lamebrains find themselves behind bars because they are so good at being so bad in their illegal activities.

Their outrageous, ridiculous, and mortifying examples of incompetence have brought disgrace to themselves and to the memories of infamous bad guys who did time in notorious lockups, from Alcatraz to Sing Sing.

These imprisoned imbeciles are too bungling to ever make the FBI's Ten Most Wanted list or be named in a police department's all-points bulletin. Nevertheless, they deserve recognition, if only for their denseness. Well, they now have their own special distinction—as members of the Dumb Crooks Hall of Shame.

There is no actual museum or building dedicated to criminal craziness. If there were such an institution, it would probably stretch several blocks to accommodate all the awards and memorabilia for the goofs and gaffes, bloopers and blunders that burglars, thieves, robbers, and other wrongdoers have committed over the years.

Even though no such brick-and-mortar gallery of dishonor exists, this book attempts to shame a relatively recent sampling of some of the jaw-droppingest, eye-poppingest, head-slappingest (yes, these are made-up words illegal in the State of Grammar) moments ever perpetrated by preposterous perpetrators.

The selection process for induction into the hall involved certain standards. All the stories had to be true and come from police files, court documents, and trusted media accounts. For each nitwit up for consideration, the author asked such questions as "Will the story make the reader laugh?" and "Is it so outlandish or silly that the reader will shake his or her head in disbelief?" If the answer was yes to those questions, then it had an excellent chance of making the cut.

Among the criminal misfits inducted into the Dumb Crooks Hall of Shame, you will read about: the knucklehead who was easily recognized and captured because he covered his face in a see-through plastic bag during a robbery . . . the foolish fugitive who was nabbed fifteen minutes after taunting the police on Facebook . . . the dense purse snatcher who knocked himself unconscious when he sprinted into a glass window that he thought was an open doorway . . . the brainless bank robber who was arrested the day after she posted a YouTube video of herself bragging about her crime . . . the idiot who, while running from police, climbed a fence and landed on the other side, not knowing it was a prison yard . . . and the loser who tried, and failed miserably, to carjack a minivan—one full of members of a judo club.

In some ways, it's easy to understand how these buffoons ended up in such disrepute. If you have crooked thoughts, it's hard to think straight.

THE "WITLESS WONDER" AWARDS

For failing to show a lick of common sense, the Dumb Crooks Hall of Shame inducts the following:

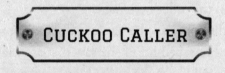

CUCKOO CALLER

BANK ROBBERY

This crook was under the harebrained assumption that robbing a bank was no different from phoning in an order for a pizza pickup. So he called a teller ten minutes ahead of time, demanding that the bank have money waiting for him and his accomplice to steal.

You might say this was a judgment call—one based on bad judgment.

The twenty-seven-year-old mastermind (please read that word with sarcasm) called a branch of the People's United Bank in Fairfield, Connecticut, one afternoon in 2010 and told a teller, "I want a hundred thousand dollars in large bills and no dye packs. I will be sending someone into the bank to get the money. Don't call the police. We are monitoring the police scanner."

After the call ended, the teller ignored his threat because, well, what crook would be dumb enough to warn the bank ahead of time that he's going to rob it? The teller immediately phoned police. Meanwhile, bank employees tried to lock the doors before the accomplice—who turned out to be the caller's sixteen-year-old cousin—showed up. But they were too late. The teen was already inside the bank and had placed a briefcase on the teller's counter.

The caller phoned the bank again and spoke to a supervisor. He asked her if she saw his "associate." When she replied yes, he said, "Don't make a scene because we will take hostages."

Once again, the caller wasn't taken that seriously. A teller put only nine hundred dollars and a dye pack in the briefcase. At the teenager's request—witnesses said he was very polite—he was let out of the bank. He then ran to a nearby parking lot, where the caller was waiting in a car.

Also waiting nearby was a police officer. With his gun drawn, he ordered them to freeze. One of the perps threw the money onto the ground just as the dye pack exploded, coloring the cash in red. The duo surrendered after other cops surrounded the car. Inside the vehicle, officers found a radio scanner tuned to the Fairfield

Police Department's frequency, two walkie-talkies, and a robbery to-do list that included times for getting into and out of the bank.

The teenager was sent to a juvenile detention facility. His older "genius" cousin eventually pleaded guilty to conspiracy to commit second-degree robbery, being a persistent dangerous felony offender, and harassment. He faced nine years in prison. Perhaps that will be a wake-up call for him.

"You can't make this stuff up," Police Sergeant James Perez told the *Connecticut Post*. "They literally called the bank and said to have the bag of money ready on the floor because they're coming to rob the place. And then they actually show up as the police are rolling in. I would classify these individuals as 'not too bright.' They should have spent time in school instead of trying to rob a bank."

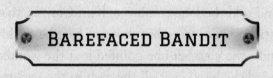

BAREFACED BANDIT

ROBBERY

No one will ever confuse this pinhead with being a master of disguise. To hide his identity during a robbery of a gas station, he wore a plastic bag over his head—a see-through plastic bag.

Was it any wonder that a cop instantly recognized him in the street from the security footage taken at the scene of the crime?

The forty-one-year-old knucklehead and his twenty-year-old pal were sitting in a home in Bethel, Cornwall, England, when they decided to rob a gas station/convenience store in nearby St. Austell in 2012. Because they didn't have masks or hoodies to conceal their faces, they grabbed the nearest things they could find. A few steps from the store, the younger one wrapped a scarf over his head, covering everything but his eyes. For some unfathomable reason, the older one chose to hide his face in a clear plastic bag.

Neither crook had a weapon, but the younger simpleton came up with what he thought was as brilliant an idea as the transparent bag. He would use his cell phone as a pretend gun.

With their so-called disguises, the pair entered the store and told the lone employee, Kim Clowes, that this was a stickup. Covering his phone as best he could with his hands, the younger one pointed it at the worker and demanded she hand over all the cash in the register. Too bad at that very moment the screen on his phone lit up.

Realizing that the man with the scarf around his head was not wielding a pistol but only a harmless cell phone, Clowes pressed a button that set off the alarm. Meanwhile, Mr. Clear Plastic Bag on His Head jumped

4

over the counter and wrestled with her. The two culprits then snared several bottles of booze and ran off.

When police arrived, they studied video from the security camera. The bagman's face was easily visible through the see-through disguise. His image was then distributed among police. Two days later, off-duty Detective Constable Lauren Holley was driving her mother home when she spotted the suspect on the street and recognized him as the dummy in the video. After she called for backup, he was arrested, and so was his birdbrained buddy.

In 2013, the two were convicted of the robbery and sentenced to two years behind bars. Detective Constable Steve White, who investigated the case, said the robber's transparent disguise was the most "ridiculous" one he had ever seen. The British media had a field day with the story on their websites. Next to a screenshot of the security video showing the nitwit wearing the clear plastic bag, the websites asked similar questions. The *Daily Mail*: "Is this Britain's stupidest crook?" Metro.co.uk: "Worst disguise ever?" The *Sun*: "Britain's daftest criminal?"

The answers: yes, yes, and yes.

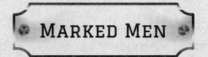

MARKED MEN

ATTEMPTED BURGLARY

These two blockheaded burglars were quick on the draw but slow on the uptake. They didn't mess with ski masks or stockings over their heads to hide their identity. Nope. They tried to disguise themselves by drawing beards and mustaches on their faces with permanent markers.

In 2009, witnesses in Carroll, Iowa, called police and reported seeing two men in hooded jackets and with black ink scribbled all over their faces trying to break into a residence. The suspects left before police responded to the attempted burglary. However, the cops were given a good description of the getaway car. A short while later, police pulled over a car matching the description of the suspects' vehicle, a 1994 Buick Roadmaster. The cops were startled—and amused—to see the men had drawn fake beards, mustaches, and streaks on their faces. Trying to explain why they marked up their mugs made the suspects, in a way, *con artists*.

"The officers were kind of laughing at the time," Carroll police chief Jeff Cayler told CNN. "I've never heard of coloring your face with a permanent marker."

In an understatement, the chief added, "They probably were just not thinking straight. [They were] being dumb."

Authorities didn't need to have a picture drawn to determine the pair was up to no good. The marked men were charged with second-degree attempted burglary.

Because their mug shots, which were taken with the permanent marker still scrawled on their faces, went viral, Cayler was fielding calls from news media outlets throughout the country. "I've been chief here almost twenty-five years, been with the department twenty-eight-and-a-half years, and I've seen a lot of weird things that make me laugh," he told CNN. "But this was probably the best combination of the two—strangely weird and hilariously funny all at the same time."

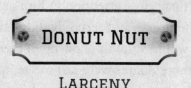

DONUT NUT

LARCENY

You would think that if you're on the run from the cops, the last thing you'd want to do is compete against them in a donut-eating contest. But then, you're not this Hall of Shamer.

He not only entered the competition, he won it! Naturally, his achievement garnered a photo and story in the local paper—a paper read by the police, who then realized the winner of their contest was really the larcenous loser who had eluded arrest for nine months. They nabbed him the next day.

The twenty-four-year-old lunkhead, who was from Elizabeth City, North Carolina, had been wanted for several felony break-ins in Camden County in 2013. The cops couldn't find him, and word on the street was that he had skipped town.

In 2014, the Elizabeth City Police Department held a National Night Out Against Crime event, which included a donut-eating contest featuring several competitors from local law enforcement agencies. Whether it was out of sheer audacity or a deep-fried love for donuts, the numbskull entered the tournament. The officers didn't pay close attention to him or the other civilian competitors—and certainly didn't think that a wanted man would stupidly show up in their midst.

Ah, but those donuts were just too tempting for this fugitive. After downing eight glazed donuts in two minutes, he was crowned the champion. The local newspaper, the *Daily Advance*, ran a story about his victory—and that's when authorities recognized him and discovered he was back in town. Deputies for the Camden County Sheriff's Office found him at his mother's residence and arrested him.

"When I came in that morning and read that article, I was [angry] because it's like throwing it in our face," Lieutenant Max Robeson told local TV station MyFox8. "We've been looking for [him] for months. I didn't ask him if he won a trophy. He probably did."

Robeson said that after the crook was arrested, "I did congratulate him" on winning the contest. "Good for him. He can eat a lot of donuts. Good for him."

Authorities *donut* know if the fugitive had a *glazed* expression when he was apprehended.

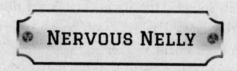

NERVOUS NELLY

ATTEMPTED BANK ROBBERY

Robbing a bank requires nerves of steel. The only nerves possessed by this would-be bank robber were made of jelly. He was so jumpy and scared that he foiled his own crime with a blunder that startled everyone—including himself.

Wearing sunglasses and a flat cap, the stocky, unshaven young man walked into a branch of Halifax Bank in London in 2011. He had hidden a gun in one hand and clutched an empty bag in the other. When he reached the teller's window, he showed the weapon and demanded the cashier put 700,000 pounds (about 870,000 dollars) in the bag.

So far, so good. But then he royally messed up. The Nervous Nelly placed on the counter what he thought was the empty bag for the money. Instead, he unthinkingly handed the bank employee the gun! There was a momentary pause when the teller and crook froze in disbelief. *Did I just give the teller my gun?* the robber thought. *Did the robber just give me his gun?* the teller thought.

Seconds later, they both made a grab for the weapon. Witnessing the goofy gaffe, bank employees immediately sounded the alarm. The jittery thief was so flustered that he fled, pedaling off on a bicycle that he had stolen from a bank worker on the way out.

A source for the City of London Police told the *Telegraph*, "The guess is that he is very inexperienced and panicked when he approached the cashier, handing over his gun instead of a bag by mistake. This man is not the sharpest tool in the box."

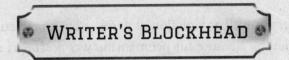

WRITER'S BLOCKHEAD

ATTEMPTED BANK ROBBERY

You might think penmanship doesn't matter, but it does. A sloppily written sentence could lead to a prison sentence.

According to police in Antioch, California, in 2014, this half-wit walked into a branch of Wells Fargo Bank, went over to a teller, and handed her a nine-word note that he had scribbled. Without saying anything, he stood there while she read the note—or at least tried to read it. The problem was, she couldn't make out what it said because his handwriting was so bad.

The customer wasn't talking, so the teller excused herself and asked her manager to help decipher the note. Together, the two bank employees determined that the note said, in a very ungrammatical way, "This is a bank robbery hand all over money."

By the time they figured out the man's intentions, the loon had seen the writing on the wall: He was not going to pull off this robbery. He bolted out through the bank's rear door. Although no money was taken, an employee called police.

Based on a detailed description of the suspect and security-camera images, police found the perp at a nearby shopping center and arrested him for attempted robbery as well as violation of parole from a previous conviction. Because his penmanship was *nothing to write home about*, he now had the time behind bars to try to *write this wrong*.

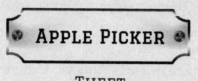

APPLE PICKER

THEFT

You've heard the expression "What goes around, comes around"? Some call it karma. After this ethics-challenged teen stole an iPhone, he had it stolen from him. But rather than chalk it up as a business loss, the moron went to the police. Want to guess how that worked out for him?

In big cities like New York, thieves have been snatching iPhones right out of the hands of vulnerable victims in a crime dubbed "Apple picking."

One day in 2013, in New York's Prospect Park, a teenage boy in pink tennis shoes grabbed an iPhone 4S from a sixteen-year-old girl and ran off with it. She reported the theft to two police officers from the Seventy-Eighth Precinct who were in a squad car.

Now here's where the karma comes into play: Shortly after the theft, the boy tried to sell the iPhone to a man on the street. The man then did to the boy what the boy had done to the girl—he yanked it out of the teen's hands and sprinted away with it.

Now here's where the stupidity comes into play: Rather than admit to himself that he was a thief who got what was coming to him, our Hall of Shamer viewed himself as a victim. He wanted justice. So he flagged down a police car and reported that a man had stolen his iPhone 4S. The boy conveniently forgot to mention that he himself had originally stolen it from a girl.

The cops found the man who had grabbed the iPhone from the boy and detained him. Then they brought the two of them to the Seventieth Precinct station house for further questioning.

Meanwhile, the victimized girl was still with the officers from the Seventy-Eighth Precinct. One of them called the girl's phone and, pretending to be its owner, asked the person who answered to return it. The person on the other end was actually an officer from the Seventieth Precinct, who was still quizzing the boy and the man.

A minute into the conversation, the two officers identified themselves to each other. Realizing that the so-called victim in the station house was most likely a thief himself, the cops came up with a plan. The officers from the Seventy-Eighth brought the girl to the Seventieth Precinct station, where she pointed to the boy in pink tennis shoes as the culprit. She proved the phone was hers by punching in the PIN to unlock it. The boy, who still claimed the phone was his, was unable to unlock it.

Officers returned the phone to its rightful owner and arrested the thief and the thief who stole it from the thief. As for the teenage culprit, well, he learned that karma is like a rubber band. You can stretch it only so far before it comes back and smacks you.

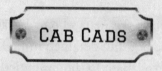

CAB CADS

BURGLARY

Memo to burglars: Hiring a taxi as your getaway car isn't smart. But if you're dumb enough to do it anyway, never stiff the driver. Not paying the cabbie means you will suffer an unwanted payback.

That certainly was the case for these two buffoons in Monmouth County, New Jersey.

According to the Deal (New Jersey) Police Department, the two suspects hailed a taxi in Asbury Park and directed the driver to a house in Deal late one night in 2016. When they arrived at the address, they told the cabbie to wait. They went inside the residence and emerged several minutes later with a television and several bottles of liquor. They got into the cab and had the driver take them to the front of their apartment building in Asbury Park.

Their plan had worked to perfection. Now all they had to do was pay the cabbie the fare, and he would be on his way, apparently oblivious to the crime they had just committed. But *noooo*. After getting out of the taxi with their stolen items, the two goons refused to pay the driver and left him fuming mad. Not smart. They had just angered the one person who had the addresses of the house they had just burglarized and their own residence.

Not surprisingly, the cabbie called police. After law enforcement officers confirmed that the house in Deal had been broken into, they went to the address in Asbury Park, where they arrested the two burglars, who were in possession of the stolen TV and liquor bottles. The items were returned to the homeowner.

The suspects were taken to Monmouth County Jail and charged with burglary, conspiracy to commit burglary, criminal trespass, and theft. As for the taxi driver, turnabout is *fare pay*.

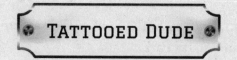

TATTOOED DUDE

BURGLARY

Sporting distinctive tattoos on your face and neck makes a statement and often draws attention. That can be good—unless you're a burglar. If you don't want to be easily identified, you might want to rethink that body ink.

The thought likely didn't cross the mind of this twenty-five-year-old lamebrain from Greenacres, Florida. He had a tattoo of the outline of the state of Florida inked onto his temple by his left eye and the word *REDRUM*—which is *MURDER* spelled backward—drawn on the left side of his neck. Those aren't common everyday tattoos.

It didn't take the cops long to identify the suspect who broke into a house in 2016 near West Palm Beach, Florida, and stole two watches and a handgun. Surveillance video clearly showed a burglar with tats of Florida and *REDRUM* on the left side of his face and neck, respectively. The homeowner told police he recognized the intruder on the video from his tattoos. The suspect was the friend of the victim's former roommate who had been to the residence before.

Investigators used a tattoo database from the Palm Beach County Jail and driver's license records and matched them to the burglar who had been released from prison after serving eight months of a yearlong sentence for felony gun and robbery convictions. For the break-in, the tat rat was arrested on charges of burglary, grand theft, and possession of a weapon by a felon.

Yep, thanks to those tattoos, he had *guilt written all over him.*

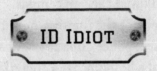

ID Idiot

PHONY BOMB THREAT

For most people, caller ID is a helpful convenience. Not so much for criminals.

In 2014 in Hayden, Idaho, this twenty-five-year-old fugitive was holed up inside his home because he knew that members of the North Idaho Violent Crimes Task Force were outside, staking out his residence. The officers, who weren't sure he was home, had a warrant for his arrest.

He needed a plan to escape, but how could he get past the cops? Then it dawned on him: He would call in a phony bomb threat to a school, which would divert officers to the scene. That way he could flee. Brilliant! Or so he thought.

Early in the afternoon, he called Atlas Elementary

School in Hayden and said someone had placed a bomb there. Within minutes, students and staff were evacuated from the campus while law enforcement officers from the Kootenai County Sheriff's Office, Coeur d'Alene Police Department, and Idaho State Police responded along with crews from Northern Lakes Fire, according to radio station KXLY. Authorities swept the interior and exterior of the school without finding any devices, so students and staff were allowed back on campus.

Unfortunately for the fugitive, he suffered an identity crisis. You see, police already knew who was responsible for the bomb hoax. When the dimwit had phoned in the phony threat, he had forgotten to block his caller ID. So his phone number had shown up on the call. Much to his chagrin—and authorities' delight—the number was easily traced to his landline at his home.

His plan to con police with a fake bomb threat *blew up* and left a lasting impact on him because he had unwittingly confirmed to members of the task force that he was still home. Moments later, they barged inside and arrested him on an unrelated felony charge as well as new charges for making a false report of a bomb at a school and obstructing an officer.

Thanks to caller ID, the dope made a name for himself.

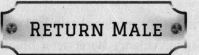

RETURN MALE

GRAND LARCENY

Seasoned crooks know that one of the most important rules in lawbreaking is don't return to the scene of the crime and try to commit it again—especially minutes later. Not being a seasoned crook, this chump didn't know that rule. Or have common sense.

In 2012, the twenty-eight-year-old dunce of the day from East Syracuse, New York, went into a branch of Alliance Bank in Syracuse and demanded twenty thousand dollars from a teller. At first, the teller refused because the would-be robber never showed a weapon or made a threat. He just kept insisting that he wanted twenty grand. Finally, the teller, who was worried that the situation could spiral out of control, caved and put cash in a bag and gave it to him.

As the perp hurried out of the bank with the money, the teller summoned police. When the robber was in a safe place, he looked in the bag and counted the money. To his outrage, he discovered the teller had shortchanged him big-time. There wasn't anything close to the twenty thousand dollars that he had demanded; there was only eleven hundred dollars. He felt he had been cheated—and he planned to do something about it.

So against all conventional criminal wisdom, he marched back to Alliance Bank determined to collect the rest of the money. But the front door was locked. And the police were inside investigating. Nevertheless, he still knocked, so they opened the door, saw he was the perp, and arrested him.

A year later, he pleaded guilty in court to fourth-degree grand larceny and was sentenced to a year in prison. Perhaps if he had thought twice about it, he wouldn't have gone twice to the bank. It led to nothing but *diminishing returns*.

PIZZA MAN

FIRST-DEGREE ROBBERY

There's one thing we know for sure about this nutbar: He's no criminal genius. How else to explain why he would phone in an order to a pizza joint and give his address—and then, when it arrived at his home, assist in robbing the delivery driver of all his pizzas and money?

This pizza scheme didn't pan out.

In about as much time as it took for the pizza to arrive, the bonehead was arrested by officers from the Tuscaloosa (Alabama) Police Department in 2014.

Sergeant Brent Blankley told the *Tuscaloosa News*

that a driver went to a mobile home one night to deliver a pizza that had been ordered for that address. When he knocked on the door, several men armed with handguns demanded all his money, all the pizzas in his car, and his wallet. The driver did what he was told, but made sure to get a good look at them. Then the robbers fled.

After police were alerted, officers went to the mobile home park and asked residents if they knew anyone who matched the descriptions given by the victim. The neighbors all mentioned the dude who lived in the mobile home where the driver was sent to deliver the pizza.

Officers went to the residence and encountered the twenty-year-old suspect, who had returned to his home. He matched the driver's description. A search of his mobile home turned up the stolen pizzas and the warming bag they were in. He was charged with first-degree robbery while his buddies were being sought on a similar charge.

Blankley told the newspaper, "We don't typically see a suspect call a delivery driver to their actual address to commit a robbery." The culprit had an *address* problem that the police *addressed*.

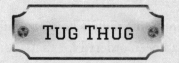

TUG THUG

ATTEMPTED BURGLARY

What can you say about a crook who can't read signs? Maybe he's too dense for a life of crime. Or maybe he was born *under a bad sign*—"out to lunch."

A surveillance camera at the Shambles Bar in Chicago showed what happened when this bumbling burglar became increasingly frustrated after he kept tugging and tugging at an unlocked door that wouldn't open.

Bar owner Joe Lin and WBBM-TV reporter Mike Parker watched seven minutes of video of the stooge's attempted burglary in 2014. "He's looking through the glass to see if there's anyone inside," said Lin. "He has a tool, so he's obviously prepared and done it before."

Within two minutes, the burglar destroys the lock. Now it should be easy to open the door. Over and over again, he pulls on the door with all his might. The jarring knocks over a security bar planted inside against the glass door. He continues to pull and tug but, mystifyingly—at least to him—he still can't get it to open. After five minutes of struggle, he finally gives up and leaves.

The dunderhead would have easily entered through the door . . . if only he had noticed the one-word sign on it that said PUSH.

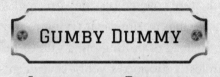

GUMBY DUMMY

ATTEMPTED ROBBERY

Hey, crooks: Don't bother robbing a convenience store dressed up as Gumby. You not only will look like a fool, you actually will be a fool.

Learn from this numbskull who, while in a full-size Gumby costume, suffered a cartoonish fail while trying to rob a 7-Eleven in the San Diego, California, suburb of Rancho Peñasquitos one night in 2011. An accomplice had driven him there after the wannabe robber had donned the bulky head-to-toe green costume of the famous Claymation humanlike character.

When this Gumby walked into the store, he announced he had a gun and demanded the store clerk give him all the money in the cash register. The clerk found it hard to take Gumby seriously. After all, what criminal dresses up like that? Believing it was all a bad joke, the annoyed clerk said he was cleaning up and didn't have time for such nonsense, Detective

Gary Hassen of the San Diego Police Department told KGTV.

According to Hassen, Gumby told the clerk, "You don't think this is a robbery? I have a gun!" Gumby, whose hands were covered by thick green gloves, fumbled inside his costume as if trying to retrieve something. Instead of pulling out a gun (if he even had one), he carelessly dropped twenty-seven cents on the floor.

Looking at the store's surveillance video later, Hassen said Gumby "can't pick up the money, and he can't get the gun." The lunkhead's accomplice then pulled up in a minivan in front of the store and honked. Gumby left the store in defeat and got into the vehicle, which took off into the night.

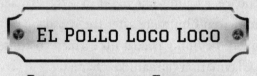

El Pollo Loco Loco

BREAKING AND ENTERING

Maybe if burglars had a dress code—like wearing only black with a ski mask—they wouldn't suffer the same fate as this doofus.

In the early morning hours in 2014, the crook broke into an El Pollo Loco in Costa Mesa, California. The restaurant's security camera caught him ransacking the eatery while looking for cash. Not finding any money, he left. When employees arrived, they looked at the video and saw that the burglar was wearing a bright green shirt and a neon-and-black hat with a picture of Animal, a character from the Muppets.

Later the same day, our Hall of Shamer had a hankering for some Mexican fire-grilled chicken. Hmm, where should he go? Yes, of course. The place he broke into hours earlier—El Pollo Loco in Costa Mesa. So he did. Oh, darn. He forgot to do one thing before he went to the restaurant—change his clothes.

So when he went up to the counter to order, the employees noticed he was wearing a bright green shirt and an Animal cap just like the burglar had on in the surveillance video. The workers wondered, *What are the odds that a customer would be wearing the exact same things as the burglar?* There's not a number high enough. They called the cops, who came and arrested the suspect before he had a chance to eat his grill-fried meal.

No winner, winner, chicken dinner for him.

THE "INTERNET REGRET"
★ PRIZES ★

For getting arrested for a crime that the perpetrator foolishly bragged about on social media, the Dumb Crooks Hall of Shame inducts the following:

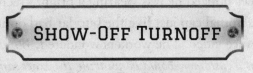
SHOW-OFF TURNOFF

BANK ROBBERY

What's the surest way to get caught after stealing a car and robbing a bank? Why, posting a video on YouTube boasting about your crimes, of course. How dumb is that? Just ask this half-witted gal, although you'll have to visit her in prison.

In 2012, the nineteen-year-old woman from Stromsburg, Nebraska, made up her mind to rob a bank. First, she peered into parked vehicles until she spotted a Pontiac Grand Am with the keys inside. She hopped in and drove it home, where she wrote out a note, put a pellet gun in her backpack, and grabbed a pillowcase. Then she took the stolen car to the nearby town of Waco, Nebraska, and parked it in front of the Cornerstone Bank.

Donning a stocking cap and sunglasses, she walked into the bank and handed a teller the note, which said, "You are being robbed! NO ALARMS OR LOCKS OR PHONES OR INK BAGS! I have a loaded gun. You have 2 minutes."

The frightened teller stuffed more than six thousand dollars in the pillowcase and handed it to the robber, who ran out of the bank and took off in the stolen vehicle. She was in and out of the bank in under a minute. For a novice like her, that was pretty impressive.

In fact, she thought it was so impressive that she felt compelled to crow about it to the world by making a nearly eight-minute video and uploading it to YouTube. She titled the video *Chick Bank Robber* and wrote in its description, "I just stole a car and robbed a bank. Now I'm rich, I can pay off my college financial aid, and tomorrow I'm going for a shopping spree."

Sitting on the floor of her bedroom, she doesn't speak during the video but instead holds up hand-written signs about her crimes. She starts the video, which uses music from the rock group Green Day as its soundtrack, by showing the sign, "I stole a car!" Then she waves the car keys. In a succession of signs, she says:

"The shiny new car is a Pontiac Grand Am. Of course I already took the license plates off and threw them out." "Then I robbed a bank!" "With a gun, a pillowcase, and a note." Smiling giddily, she waves a thick wad of the 6,256 dollars she has just stolen. While she fans out the bills, a subtitle says, "I told my mom today was the best day of my life :) She just thinks I met a new boy." Next, she fans her face with hundred-dollar bills.

If she wanted notoriety, she got it. The video went viral, with more than 1.7 million views. Among those who saw it were the cops. The next morning, deputies from the York and Polk County sheriff's departments arrested her at her home. She was still wearing the same clothes—striped shirt and dark pants—that she wore during the video and the robbery. Deputies recovered the stolen vehicle and all but thirty dollars of the bank's money.

She later told a reporter for Omaha, Nebraska, TV station WOWT, "I was very proud of myself having the guts to do what I did." When she learned that her video was a YouTube hit, she said, "I didn't know it was going to get popular."

After pleading guilty to bank robbery, she was sentenced by a York County judge to ten to twenty years in prison. She told the judge, "I shouldn't have robbed a bank." She added, "I learned that robbing a bank takes you to jail." And making a video boasting of your crimes takes you there that much faster.

SNAPCHAT(TERBOX)

BURGLARY

There is a time and a place to use social media. Hiding in a kitchen cabinet from the cops is neither the time nor the place, as one dumb fugitive discovered.

This twenty-four-year-old space case from Fairfield, Maine, was wanted on charges that he broke into a campground lodge in northern Somerset County and stole a propane cookstove and a cast-iron woodstove in 2015. After gathering evidence at the scene, the sheriff's office recovered the stoves, including one found in the suspect's house. But he had disappeared, so authorities asked the public for help in locating the burglar.

The best assistance law enforcement received on this case came from the jughead himself. Even though he was hiding from the cops, he couldn't stop himself from using Snapchat, the popular app that automatically deletes messages seconds after they're posted. First, he messaged that he was in his house, prompting some law-abiding recipients to call the cops. And then, while police were searching the residence, he Snapchatted again exactly where he was concealing himself. What was he thinking? Okay, he obviously wasn't.

Here, on its Facebook page, the Somerset County Sheriff's Office explained what happened:

"Over the past few weeks, since our press release looking for the public's assistance in locating him, [the suspect] had become cocky. Which led to his downfall. This is where our story picks up.

"Last night, using the Snapchat app, [the suspect] posted that he was at his house in Fairfield, which prompted people to call the Sheriff's Office. Corporal Ritchie Putnam, Deputy Ron Blodgett from our agency, and two officers from the Fairfield Police Department went to the residence. They were given permission to search the house, and initially they did not find [the suspect].

"Here's where things went bad for him: While the deputies/officers were wrapping up their search, [the suspect] posted again on Snapchat. This time he posted that the police were searching for him in the house, and that he was hiding in a cabinet. Again, we received phone calls. A search of the kitchen cabinets turned up some food, some pots and pans, and also a pair of feet. The pair of feet just so happened to be attached to a person, and that person was [the suspect]. He was removed from the cabinet and placed under arrest.

"Also arrested at the residence was a young lady . . . for hindering apprehension, because . . . well . . . let's put it this way: When the police ask you multiple times if someone is in the house, and you answer repeatedly that they are not in the house, and that you have not seen said person in 'weeks,' you're just going to get arrested. That's how it happens [when you lie]."

For the chatty offender, who was charged with burglary, theft, and violation of conditions of release, his life *changed in a snap*.

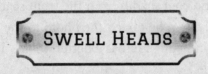

SWELL HEADS

FAILURE TO APPEAR IN COURT

I n separate cases, these two featherbrained fugitives were so vain they contacted police because they didn't like the mug shots the cops posted of them online. One of the pinheads even sent in a replacement selfie. Needless to say, their abundance of vanity and lack of sanity led to their arrests.

Case No. 1: This forty-five-year-old dummy was wanted by the Lima (Ohio) Police Department in 2016 because he failed to appear in court on a charge of driving under the influence. He was also a person of interest in separate cases involving vandalism and arson. On its Facebook page, the department posted his mug shot from a earlier arrest. The *Lima News* reported that his earlier run-ins with the police included charges of disorderly conduct, breaking and entering, and domestic violence.

When the suspect saw his mug shot on Facebook, he was upset because it wasn't flattering at all (as if any police mug shot is). So he took a selfie wearing a snazzy sport coat and cool shades from the front seat of a late-model SUV. Then he texted the photo to the cops along with this comment: "Here is a better photo. That other one is terrible."

Always trying to be accommodating to those criminals they seek to arrest, Lima police posted his selfie next to his other mug shot on their Facebook page, saying, "This photo was sent to us by [the suspect] himself. We thank him for being helpful, but now we would appreciate it if he would come speak to us at the LPD about his charges."

The department's post explained there was an active warrant for his arrest and asked for the public's help in locating the suspect. The posting of the photo received more than 3,600 likes, 4,500 shares, and 400 comments. Among them: "Arrogance has no bounds!" "Are you serious, dummy?" "Oh wow. Stupid and still a horrible photo." And this: "Dude. Stop. Trust me. You look even slimier and cheesier."

To carry his vanity even further, the suspect called an Ohio radio station—while he was still evading the cops—and explained why he texted police a selfie. "Man, they just did me wrong," he told the talk-show hosts. "They put a picture out that made me look like I was a Thundercat or James Brown on the run. I can't let them do that."

The background of the selfie showed enough for authorities to determine that the photo was taken in a late-model Infiniti crossover SUV. With all the attention the selfie garnered, it took only a week before the egotistical egghead was arrested in Century, Florida.

Following his capture, Lima police posted this Facebook shout-out to the Florida cops who nabbed him and to the public: "Thanks to the power of social media & tips called into authorities, we have learned that [the suspect] has been arrested by the Escambia County Sheriff's Office in Florida. Thank you to Escambia County & to those who provided information and continue to support law & order."

As for the suspect, well, his selfie was *all in vain*.

Case No. 2: This fugitive, who was *me-deep* in self-importance, also came from Ohio. When the Columbus Division of Police posted a mug shot of her on its Facebook page because she was wanted for aggravated robbery and other serious charges, she was outraged. What upset her more than the charges was her photo, which she felt was too unflattering.

Officers were looking for her in 2014 after she was accused of pulling a gun on an acquaintance and robbing her. The department posted the woman's mug shot from a previous arrest. Two days after the photo appeared on Facebook, the suspect called the cops, insisting they delete her picture because it was such an unattractive shot.

"This is a first for us," Denise Alex-Bouzounis, the police department's public information officer, told the Huffington Post. "She really didn't want her face out there for everyone to see. She contacted the detective listed on the Facebook post and said, 'Hey, I want my picture down.' [The detective] said, 'Come on in, and we'll talk about it.'"

Surprisingly, the nitwit showed up. Not surprisingly, she was arrested on the spot.

But at least the woman got her way. The Columbus Division of Police took a new mug shot of her and removed the older offending photo from its Facebook page—but not before the page had racked up more than fifty thousand views. On the page was a link to the Huffington Post story, which included the original mug shot. The department's post said, "Looks like CPD & suspect are getting some national attention. The [mug shot] she wanted taken off CPD Facebook is now seen around the US and beyond!"

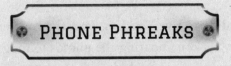

PHONE PHREAKS

THEFT

Why is there a need for iPhone thieves to snap selfies? Do they not get the *big picture* that the photos likely will lead to their arrest? Apparently not these Hall of Shamers.

Case No. 1: This twenty-year-old knucklehead swiped an iPhone in Harlem, New York, in 2013. No one knew he possessed the stolen cell phone. And no one would have known had he held his ego in check. But, no, with the victim's phone, he just had to take some selfies of his handsome face. He snapped one of himself wearing a black Lacoste hoodie and another posing in front of a vehicle while flashing gang signs. He also took a close-up in the hoodie while sporting a pair of white earbuds.

What the simpleton failed to realize was that these vanity shots automatically were uploaded to the victim's photo-sharing Apple iCloud account that stores pictures, music, and videos. When the victim saw these strange selfies, he forwarded them to police.

According to the *New York Post*, the cops ran a computer check, comparing the photos to mug shots of those who had committed similar crimes in upper Manhattan. Police easily picked out the suspect because he had been arrested for a similar robbery. Once they learned his identity, they went to his Harlem apartment and arrested him. His ego trip took him directly to jail, where he was charged with criminal possession of stolen property.

Case No. 2: These two jerks stole a teen's cell phone during a party—and then all but convicted themselves by sending a selfie to the victim's friends.

At an eighteen-and-under club in New York City in 2014, the culprits, who were teenage boys, stole an iPhone belonging to a fourteen-year-old boy. Later, on the subway, the terrible two took a picture of themselves sporting silly expressions. Then they foolishly sent it to the victim's friends—along with a vulgar message to his mother—via the photo-messaging app Snapchat.

One of the victim's pals took a screenshot of the selfie and forwarded it to the victim's mom. She, in turn, shared it with police. The cops released the photo to the media, hoping someone would recognize the two thieves.

Among the first to recognize the crooks were the

crooks themselves. They had no choice but to turn themselves in to the authorities, who charged them with petit larceny and criminal possession of stolen property.

In an understatement, the victim told the *New York Post* that by taking his phone and then a selfie, "they're pretty stupid."

Brain-wise, it's as if their phone was on, but they had no signal.

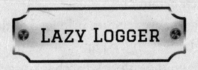

LAZY LOGGER

BURGLARY

Logging on to Facebook at work is typically a no-no. Logging on to Facebook on the computer of the home you're burglarizing and forgetting to log off is an *oh no.*

One rainy night in 2014, this blunderer broke into a residence near Minneapolis and stole money, credit cards, a cell phone, and other valuables, including an expensive watch. Rather than make a quick getaway, he lingered in the house because he just had to check his Facebook page. Right then.

He took off his rain-soaked jeans and Nike tennis shoes and sat down at the homeowner's computer. He logged on to his account and scanned Facebook. When he was finished, he put on a pair of shoes and pants owned by the victim and left the house with the stolen items. To the burglar, it was a job well done.

Later that night, the homeowner showed up and discovered that someone had broken into his house. He found a stranger's wet shoes and jeans lying on the floor. And he also noticed something else that was odd. His computer was on and it was displaying the Facebook profile of a certain "Nick Dub"—a person he had never seen before.

Assuming the wet clothes belonged to the burglar and the burglar was "Nick Dub," the victim posted a brief message on the culprit's Facebook page accusing him of being a thief. He asked anyone who read the message on Nick's page to call him (the victim) with any information about the crime. He gave out his cell phone number.

The next day, someone did respond—the burglar, who sent the surprised victim a text.

Recalling the incident, the homeowner later told WCCO-TV, "I replied, 'You left a few things at my house last night. How can I get them back to you?'"

Incredibly, the burglar agreed to meet later that evening at the residence he had broken into the night before. He was under the impression he would get back the clothes he had left in exchange for the cell phone that he had stolen.

A short while later, the victim spotted our dense Hall of Shamer walking toward the residence and recognized him from the man's Facebook profile photo. The homeowner immediately called police. Minutes after the burglar showed up to reclaim his clothes, the cops arrived and arrested him. The crook, who was wearing the victim's stolen watch, faced up to ten years in prison.

"I've never seen this before," Dakota County attorney James Backstrom told WCCO. "It's a pretty unusual case. [The burglar] might even make the late night television shows in terms of not being too bright."

As for the scoundrel, he was now logging time behind bars.

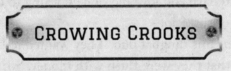

CROWING CROOKS

BANK ROBBERY

This couple boasted to the world that they were rolling in dough by posting photos of themselves on Facebook with big wads of money. There's nothing wrong with that, right? Well, there is, if one of you is an ex-con and you posted the pictures just days after a bank robbery.

The blockhead had been released from prison a

month earlier after serving time for a bank robbery in a nearby town. It makes you wonder why the convicted felon foolishly thought the cops wouldn't take a keen interest in his postings. Because they certainly did.

He set out to rob a branch of the Savings Bank in Ashville, Ohio, in 2015. Because he was so heavily tattooed—he sported the phrases "Loyalty's Thin" and "Betrayal's Thick" on opposite cheeks—he first had his girlfriend apply makeup to him to cover up the numerous tats on his face and neck.

Wearing a hoodie, he walked into the bank and gave a note demanding money to a teller, who then handed over more than six thousand dollars in cash. He ran out with the dough and into a waiting car driven by his girlfriend. They made a clean getaway. Savvy robbers would have laid low and done nothing to draw attention or suspicion.

But not this dingbat duo. They wanted to brag to everyone that they were flush with money. So, four days after the robbery, they began posting pictures of themselves on Facebook. There they are embracing while he holds fistfuls of cash. There he is pretending a pack of bills is a cell phone. Oh, and there he is in two photos with a wad of money in his mouth. "That's called a McStack," the culprit wrote on Facebook.

The pictures miffed a relative, who complained on Facebook that the suddenly cash-rich robber hadn't shared the money with family.

In another post, the robber bragged, "I'm doing rrree=aaaaalll good."

Not really. You see, the Pickaway County Sheriff's Office already considered him a top suspect because of his criminal record and witnesses' description of the robber. He had been convicted of robbing a branch of the Fairfield National Bank in nearby Lancaster, Ohio, in 2010 and had served five years in Ohio state lockup. Released only a few weeks before the Ashville robbery, he had just started a three-year parole term.

Sheriff Robert Radcliff told the *Columbus Dispatch* that the bank's surveillance camera got a good look at the robber, who had "a funny complexion and a birthmark." The sheriff added that it was obvious the crook tried to cover his tattoos with makeup.

The Facebook photos merely confirmed authorities' suspicions. Within days of the crime, sheriff's deputies nabbed the reckless birdbrains and charged them with robbery and theft. The pair eventually pleaded guilty in Pickaway County Common Pleas Court. He was sentenced to three years, and she to two. Both were ordered to pay back all the money they stole.

Their post-robbery Facebook photos went viral, causing commenters to label them "the world's dumbest criminals" for what the sheriff said was the robbers' "stone cold stupidity."

You can bank on it.

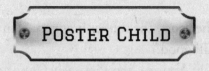

BURGLARY

This brainless burglar got caught because he made a virtual wanted poster of himself.

In 2011, he broke into the home of *Washington Post* journalist Marc Fisher and stole two laptops, four hundred dollars, and a new winter coat that hadn't even been worn yet. He just couldn't leave well enough alone. No, he wanted to rub it into the faces of the victimized family.

Writing in the *Post* about the crime, Fisher said, "He opened my son's computer, took a photo of himself sneering as he pointed to the cash lifted from my son's desk, and then went on my son's Facebook account and posted the picture for 400 teenagers to see. In the picture, the man is wearing my new winter coat, the one that was stolen right out of the Macy's box it had just arrived in."

Although the burglar wore the new coat's hood up, the picture clearly showed his face. "The gall and stupidity wrapped up in that act made our case something of a sensation," Fisher wrote. "Newspapers, websites, and TV stations from New Delhi to New England carried the story after I wrote a column about the burglary. Before DC police even assigned a detective, more than 150 news outlets had published the burglar's photo."

Police recognized him. He was a nineteen-year-old lawbreaker who had already been arrested seven times; faced criminal charges in Virginia, New York, and the District of Columbia; and had skipped out on court appearances twice—and that wasn't even counting his juvenile record.

A month after the burglary, the cops spotted him in an alley and arrested him on a burglary charge and an unrelated weapons charge. He eventually pleaded guilty in DC Superior Court and was sentenced to three and a half years in prison.

Fisher said that one police officer told him, "I've seen a lot, but this is the most stupid criminal I've ever seen."

At least this buffoon would be *out of the picture* for a while.

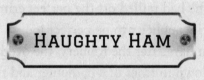

☢ HAUGHTY HAM ☢

BANK ROBBERY

This arrogant bank robber was miffed by several factual errors that police had given to the media about his crime. Because his brains were no match for his conceit, he sent the cops corrections to their report—in an email that contained his email address. No need to wonder how easily he was nabbed.

Wearing sunglasses and a cap to hide his face, he entered a bank in Röttingen, Bavaria, Germany, in 2011. After threatening a teller with a knife, he left with what police said was "several hundred euros." To the media, police released the following description of the offender: "Male, between 180 and 185 cm in height, aged 20 to 25, with short, dark hair. The man spoke with a southern Bavarian German accent." The cops also mentioned that the robber fled on foot.

The felon was peeved that the information the cops provided to the media had too many inaccuracies. He just had to set the record straight. Most criminals would be delighted if the media unwittingly publicized wrong descriptions and misinformation about their crimes because that would make them harder for police to solve. But this show-off was too self-absorbed. Because he thought he had pulled off the perfect crime, he wanted all the publicity to be perfect too.

So seven days after the robbery, the overly confident culprit sat down in front of a computer and typed out a message to the Bavarian police. First off, he boasted that he had stolen 2,500 euros and not several hundred. He said that he was nineteen years old, 193 cm tall, and born in Württemberg; that he didn't flee on foot, but escaped in a red Mercedes; that he slipped past a police checkpoint; and that he left the car in a train station's parking garage before boarding the InterCity Express to Hamburg. He also gave police hints about his location, as if daring them to find him. Mocking the authorities for getting so many things wrong, he wrote, "This is not appropriate police work."

He emailed the message to the police as well as the German newspapers *Bild* and *Main Post*. At the top of the email for all recipients to see was his real email address. Within hours, the cops in Hamburg nabbed the egomaniac.

"He was completely shocked" when he was arrested, a police spokesman told Reuters news agency. "His game of cat and mouse went all wrong."

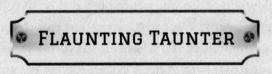

FLAUNTING TAUNTER

BURGLARY

Mocking the cops on their own police department Facebook page is never a good idea, especially if you're a wanted man. This noodle-headed burglary suspect was arrested just fifteen minutes after he posted his taunt.

Police in Rosenberg, Texas, had evidence that two brothers had burglarized seventeen cars in a neighborhood in 2013. They collared one of the suspects, but the other one remained at large. In an appeal for help from the public, authorities posted the mug shot of the wanted man on their Facebook page.

When our Hall of Shamer saw his photo on the cops' Facebook page, he just couldn't resist teasing them. He posted a profanity-laced comment to the police. In the only part that's suitable for readers, he said, ". . . im innocent, catch me if u can . . ."

So the cops took up his challenge. And they caught him. After booking him, the police responded to his taunt by posting on the department's Facebook page the suspect's photo with a caption in red that said "CAPTURED."

Below the photo, the police posted this: "Not 15 minutes after [the suspect] 'taunted' law enforcement and the community as a whole on our own Facebook site, your Rosenberg Police Officers (detectives and patrol alike) located [him] hiding out at a family member's home, where he was captured. [He] is one of two alleged suspects in the Seaborne Meadow's Burglary of Motor Vehicles case, where at least 17 of your vehicles were burglarized . . . And in a bizarre twist, the resident of the home he was hiding out in also had a warrant."

Detective Chris Juusola, who monitored the department's Facebook page, told KTBC-TV, "I wish things could be that easy all the time."

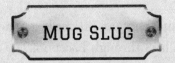

MUG SLUG

AGGRAVATED ASSAULT

Most people would be embarrassed to have their police mug shot on Facebook. Not this numbskull. He shared it with everybody. That's not necessarily worthy of Hall of Shame status, except in his case it is, because he was a fugitive at the time—and it led to his capture.

The suspect was wanted in 2013 on multiple charges, including aggravated assault stemming from an argument that got out of hand and led to a robbery. The thirty-five-year-old culprit had remained elusive until early 2014, when the Freeland (Pennsylvania) Police Department posted his mug shot on its Facebook page and asked the community for help in finding him.

Well, someone did—the dumb crook himself.

Among the dozens of people who shared the police message on Facebook was the fugitive, who reposted his mug shot on his page within three minutes of the original post. Under his picture, he added an obscenity-filled commentary that said (minus the swear words) "lol, I love it." He concluded by calling the police a bad name.

The cops saw his post and didn't take kindly to his remark. They were determined to arrest him. Posing as an attractive woman who claimed she was intrigued by the suspect's mug shot, an officer began a virtual conversation with him through Facebook.

After they traded several messages with each other over the next half hour, the fugitive agreed to meet this interesting "woman" at a specific location. When the fugitive showed up, he was greeted not by a lovely lady but by several stern cops. It was a picture-perfect arrest.

He was charged with disorderly conduct, aggravated assault, harassment, reckless endangerment, theft, and criminal mischief. Unable to post bail, he was jailed at the Luzerne County Prison.

Within two hours of the arrest, the Freeland Police Department posted the suspect's wanted photo on Facebook again, this time with the caption: "CAPTURED!!!!!! SHARES OUR STATUS ON FACEBOOK ABOUT HIMSELF, CAPTURED 45 MINUTES LATER."

THE "MURPHY'S LAW"

★ MEDALS ★

For proving that if anything can go wrong, it will, the Dumb Crooks Hall of Shame inducts the following:

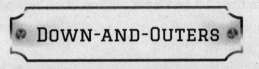

DOWN-AND-OUTERS

BREAKING AND ENTERING

Life had its *ups and downs* for these unlucky burglars. It looked like they had pulled off a major diamond heist, but fate gave them *the shaft* because, during their getaway, they got stuck in an elevator.

According to the Hamilton County (Ohio) Sheriff's Office, the fifty-seven-year-old man and his accomplice, a sixty-one-year-old woman, targeted the Diamonds Rock jewelry store in the Cincinnati suburb of Kenwood in 2015 after hours. The pair parked their rental car in the basement garage of the building where the store was located. They went to another floor, where they smashed through the front door of the store. Then the man used a crowbar and screwdriver to pry open a second door.

Once inside, the couple shattered a glass showcase and picked out more than two dozen diamond rings, pendants, and other jewelry. Because the burglars had tripped the alarm, they had only a minute or two to grab what they could—which was about eighty thousand dollars' worth of items—and flee. They were in and out before sheriff's deputies arrived.

Having snatched all that jewelry, the thieves needed to get to their car and leave the area. This was when they should have taken steps to avoid the elevator. But they didn't.

The pair hurried down the stairwell only to hit a dead end. The stairs went to a lower level, but not to the garage. Knowing that deputies had now arrived at the store, the chumps scrambled to the nearest elevator and pushed the button for the garage. The doors closed and the elevator started to move. It let them down, but not in the way they intended. Before reaching the garage, the elevator stopped and wouldn't budge. No amount of prying could spring open the shut doors. The couple was trapped, having lowered themselves to a new *level of despair*.

Resigned that they were going to need help to get out of this predicament, they first stashed the stolen jewels and burglar's tools in the ceiling of the elevator.

Then they yelled and pounded on the doors. Deputies who were investigating the break-in heard noises coming from the elevator, which was next to the business. When they discovered that two people were stuck inside, deputies called in the Sycamore Township Fire Department to free them.

The twosome had some explaining to do about why they were in an elevator in a locked building after hours. While the couple was being detained, deputies found the missing jewelry and burglar's tools in the elevator. According to Cincinnati TV station WLWT, Mike Lane, the owner of the store, was there when deputies arrested the pair. Lane snapped at the burglars, "What in the world in your mind gives you the right to think you can steal what people work so hard for?" Neither culprit responded; they remained stone-faced.

The two were initially charged with breaking and entering and possessing criminal tools.

Grateful for the faulty elevator, Sheriff Jim Neil told WLWT, "Sometimes karma makes sure things work out how they should."

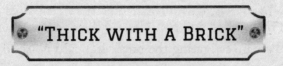

"THICK WITH A BRICK"

ATTEMPTED THEFT

The Irish press labeled this bumbling would-be thief "Thick with a Brick" for good reason. He threw a brick hoping to smash a window of a Mercedes-Benz car, but the brick rebounded off the glass, struck him in the face, and knocked him out.

"We have the whole thing on [surveillance video], and it's quite hilarious," Gerry Brady, who owned the car, told the *Irish Examiner*. Brady, owner of the Pheasant Pub in Drogheda, County Louth, Ireland, said his security camera caught all the action as he and his girlfriend were closing the tavern for the night.

"At first he throws a small stone at the [passenger's window] of my Mercedes without success," Brady told the paper after viewing the video. "He tries again with the same stone and still nothing happens." At that point, the culprit went over to Brady's girlfriend's car, which was parked nearby. He broke a window of her vehicle and took items from the glove compartment.

"But he is still determined to get into the Mercedes and walks down a lane at the side of the pub before returning with a concrete brick," Brady narrated. "He takes a run-up and really [hurls] it at the [driver's window], but unfortunately for him it rebounds and smashes him in the face, lifting him up into the air and laying him flat out.

"I'll give him this—he was determined. He had three separate goes at it. He got some smack when the brick rebounded back into his gob [face]."

Brady said he and his girlfriend discovered the man lying near the Mercedes around 1:00 a.m. "At first I didn't know what had happened," Brady told the newspaper. "[We saw] this guy lying flat on his back with blood pouring from him, so naturally enough [we] went over to help him.

"Initially I thought the poor bloke had been knocked down by a car [because] he was in such a bad way. When I asked him what had happened, he told me his mate had attacked him. I told him I was [calling] an ambulance and the [police because] he needed to report it. But he didn't seem to want the cops involved, which made me suspicious. My partner then noticed the damage to her car. I had a look at the Mercedes and could see dents on it."

The situation quickly took a threatening turn. Brady told the *Irish Independent*, "He pulled himself up and said he wanted fifty euros for a taxi. I said, 'Not a chance, mate.' That's when he leaned in and told me he'd burn me out of the pub."

Retreating to a nearby gas station, Brady and his girlfriend called the police. When officers arrived, the bloodied man claimed that Brady had attacked him.

But when Brady and the cops went into the pub and watched the video from the security cameras, the truth was plain to see.

"You should have heard [the officers] laughing when they saw the video," Brady said.

"They were in stitches." And so was our bloodied Hall of Shamer. But it was no laughing matter to him because he really needed stitches.

The *Examiner* called the culprit a contender for the country's dumbest criminal of the year.

Brady uploaded the video to YouTube. Since then more than seven million people have viewed "Thick with a Brick's" hilariously inept attempt at stealing Brady's car.

Yep, he was a real *head case*.

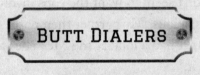

BUTT DIALERS

BURGLARY

When it comes to dumb lawbreakers, there's no accounting for carelessness. In two separate incidents in 2013, these hapless burglars were caught after they accidentally butt-dialed the cops.

Case No. 1: These two jugheads broke into a house on the outskirts of McAlester, Oklahoma, and were thrilled about what they were stealing—money, jewelry, and a gun. The crime was going so smoothly . . . until one of the crooks inadvertently pocket-dialed 911. As Pittsburg County dispatchers listened in with great interest, the crooked pair chatted about their burglary while they were still in the house—and while the phone call was still live.

"We're good," one of the burglars told the other. "I got enough jewelry. We're good."

"I didn't even get to go through half of the house," the other protested.

After they stepped out of the residence, they debated going back inside. One of them wanted to park their getaway truck in the garage. "What if something happened and they did come home, what would you do then?" one asked his partner.

While this conversation was going on, neither burglar realized the butt-dialed call was being heard by dispatchers, who had already transferred it to deputies. Authorities quickly traced the location of the cell phone and were able to confront the burglars as they tried to sell the stolen goods at a nearby pawn shop.

"Never have I seen or heard of anything like this," Pittsburg County sheriff Joel Kerns told Tulsa TV station KJRH. "Usually we have to go to the most extremes to catch someone." But unwittingly calling the one number no self-respecting criminal would ever want to call made it easy for authorities to apprehend the crooks. Kerns, an eleven-year law enforcement veteran, said the butt-dialing burglar was "one of the world's dumbest criminals."

They were held at the Pittsburg County Criminal Justice Center on a twenty-five thousand dollar bond, facing a charge of second-degree burglary.

Case No. 2: A few months earlier, these two twenty-year-old simpletons in Fresno, California, were discussing breaking into a car when one of them unknowingly butt-dialed 911. He didn't hear the dispatcher answer, "What's your emergency?"

Instead, as the dispatcher stayed on the line, the suspects continued to talk about the crime they were about to commit. "Get the bolt and give me the hammer just in case," one of the thieves said. Seconds later, the dispatcher heard a window shatter and the perps shouting with glee over what they found in the car.

The dispatcher had already alerted police, who were looking for the culprits in a certain area based on clues that the dispatcher was picking up from the pocket-dialed call. The cops eventually spotted the suspects as they were driving away from the scene of the crime.

At this point in the call, which authorities recorded, the driver told his partner, "Oh, he's following me, dog. Wow, what did I do?"

After the police pulled them over and began questioning them, the pair denied any wrongdoing. But after searching the car, officers found items that had been taken from the burglarized vehicle.

The cops handcuffed the nitwits and then told them how they'd been caught. Pointing to his partner, who had butt-dialed authorities, the burglar shook his head in disbelief and asked officers, "This fool really called 911?"

Sergeant Jaime Rios of the Fresno Police Department told the *Los Angeles Times*, "The crooks were pretty shocked when the officer told them that they had butt-dialed 911. They had no clue." Rios said the suspects were charged with burglary, conspiracy, and possession of stolen property.

To ABCNews.com, Rios added, "There have been times where the dispatcher hears something like this, but never has a call come in before a crime was committed and [the call] stays on all the way to the end."

For the two who were arrested, the less said about it, the *butt-er*.

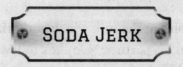

SODA JERK

ATTEMPTED THEFT

This birdbrained teenager tried to steal a soda from a vending machine and discovered that crime doesn't pay. In fact, it can be costly.

In 2012, the seventeen-year-old skateboarder stopped at the trolley station in National City, a suburb of San Diego, California, around 5:00 a.m. and tried to grab a soda from a Coca-Cola vending machine without paying for it. He sat on the floor and stuck his left hand up the slot where the cans of soda drop. When he couldn't quite reach a can, he twisted and shoved his whole left arm up into the guts of the machine. Still no luck.

The bad boy finally gave up. But when he tried to get his arm out, it was wedged in so tightly that he couldn't move it. He was *sodaspondent*. Finally, an early-morning trolley rider spotted the stuck teen and called police.

Summoned to the scene were firefighters, police, paramedics, and trolley security, leaving the high schooler with mixed emotions—embarrassment from being caught in this predicament and relief that he would soon be rescued. But the word *soon* was relative. No one had the key to unlock the soda machine, which meant the rescue would require a lengthy effort.

According to NBCSanDiego.com, authorities began using axes to chop at the sides of the vending machine. When that method failed, rescuers tried wielding crowbars—also to no avail.

Firefighters then brought in a special rotary saw and hydraulic chisel, which cut and broke apart the inside of the vending machine until the teen was freed.

The entire rescue took about an hour. "Medics at the scene treated the teen for scrapes and soreness to his arm caused by numerous attempts to free himself," NBCSanDiego.com reported. "The teen was taken into custody by police, who said he may face charges for petty theft. Authorities said the teen might also have to foot the bill for fire and medical services, as well as damages to the soda machine. In the end, the teenager never got his soda."

That soft drink he wanted led to a hard lesson.

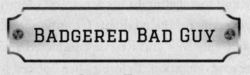

BADGERED BAD GUY

AUTO THEFT

This doofus played a serious game of hide-and-seek with the police—and lost.

When officers tried to make a traffic stop in Ontario, Oregon, in 2016, two suspects in a stolen SUV sped off. The thieves, who had their dog with them, eventually ditched the vehicle and ran into a remote area supervised by the Bureau of Land Management.

Our Hall of Shamer thought he had found the perfect place to conceal himself—deep inside a badger hole. Fortunately, the badger wasn't home. Unfortunately, the crook became stuck headfirst. He had squeezed himself in so firmly that he couldn't budge.

Meanwhile, during a foot search of the area, police nabbed his buddy, who was smart enough not to hide in the home of a nocturnal mammal from the weasel family. Cops then followed the dog, which scampered right into the hole. When they tried to coax the dog to come out, they heard the twenty-two-year-old idiot screaming for help.

After discovering that he was stuck eight feet underground in the badger hole and suffering from exposure and lost feeling in his arms, the Ontario Police Department, the Malheur County Sheriff's Office, and Vale Fire and Rescue conducted a ninety-minute rescue operation. Before police booked him on multiple charges, he was taken to Saint Alphonsus Medical Center in Ontario, where he was treated for minor injuries.

Although he was no longer in the badger hole, he now found himself in a bigger hole—the one that he had dug for himself.

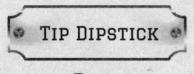

TIP DIPSTICK

THEFT

This flake stole a restaurant's tip jar and came out poorer from the experience. He actually lost money on his crime.

The simpleton came into Nando's, an eatery in Christchurch, New Zealand, in 2015 and went up to the counter. He paid fourteen dollars and ninety cents for a meal and then sat down to wait for his food. When no one was looking, he went over to the tip jar, slipped it and the money into his bag, and headed for the bathroom.

Restaurant owner Yateen Lallu was alerted to the theft when his wife noticed the tip jar was missing. She pointed to the man, who had just returned from the bathroom. Lallu confronted the suspect, who denied any wrongdoing. Lallu then checked the bathroom and discovered the empty tip jar on the floor.

Lallu later told Stuff.co.nz, "I said to him, 'There's our tip jar.' And he said, 'It wasn't me. It must have been someone else.' I said, 'Are you sure? Are you telling the truth?' And he told me to check his bag and check the security cameras, so I started to doubt myself."

Lallu went into a back room and looked at the security-camera footage. It clearly showed the man had indeed taken the tip jar and money. But by the time Lallu returned to the front of the restaurant, the thief was gone, having left poorer and hungrier than when he had entered the place.

"He hadn't gotten his food, so he paid fourteen dollars and ninety cents for something he didn't get," Lallu said. "In total, he probably got five to ten dollars from the tip jar. So it wasn't worth it. He had a bad day."

The only *tip* that the thief should have taken was, "Hey, jerk, don't steal!"

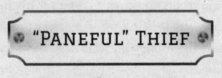

"PANEFUL" THIEF

PURSE SNATCHING

It wouldn't be a stretch to say that this purse snatcher's crime was a *knockout*. The knucklehead KO'd himself when he ran straight through what he thought was an open glass door. It wasn't.

The thief was lurking by a store in a busy shopping mall in Perth, Australia, in 2013, waiting for the right victim. He spotted his target, a fifty-year-old woman who had no idea the lanky young man was about to strike.

He eyed the woman and then checked out his getaway route. There, off to his left, was a wide corridor leading to an automatic glass door. All he had to do was run up from behind the woman, grab her purse, and dash outside.

In a flash, he snatched the victim's handbag and sprinted down the corridor toward the door. No one stopped him, and it looked like clear sailing for him.

While he was running, he made a slight miscalculation. The automatic door slid open from right to left so that the opening was on the right. To the left of the door was a floor-to-ceiling plate-glass window with a large potted plant in front to keep people from doing what the thief was seconds away from doing.

Thinking the automatic door was open when, in fact, it was closed, and failing to pay any attention to the potted plant directly in front of him, the thief slammed smack into the thick plate-glass window at full speed. As a security-camera video showed, he knocked himself unconscious on impact. He struck the pane so hard it spider-webbed, flew out of its frame, and fell to the ground, with the bozo landing flat on his face on top of it.

Bystanders who were unaware of the purse snatching came to his aid. When he finally regained consciousness, people tried to help him to his feet. Dazed and confused, he started crawling on his hands and knees until an accomplice showed up and dragged him to a waiting car. The vehicle, which had been reported stolen, sped off. The thief ended up with the purse—and a splitting headache.

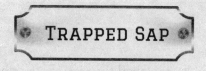

BURGLARY

Sometimes crooks make things more difficult than they have to be. This Hall of Shamer tried to gain entry into a house not by the usual method of breaking a window or jimmying a door. Nope, he tried going down the chimney.

That might work for Santa Claus, but it sure didn't work for this chimney creep. Ho-ho-ho turned into *oh-no-no* because he got stuck. In fact, he was squeezed in so tightly that he needed the fire department to rescue him just so the cops could arrest him.

According to the Ridgecrest (California) Police Department, the bonehead and a woman accomplice plotted a late-night burglary of the residence in 2017. The plan called for him to enter the house through the chimney and then open the door for his partner. He climbed onto the roof and began sliding down the chimney—and quickly became trapped. No matter how hard he wriggled and twisted, he couldn't move up or down.

Hoping to free him from below, his accomplice burst into the house by forcing open the back door. But by doing so, she triggered the burglar alarm. Trying to save her own skin and showing no loyalty to her pitiful partner, she dashed out of the house and disappeared, leaving him dangling in the air. When the police arrived, they were unaware that he was stuck in the chimney. But then a call came in to 911 from an anonymous woman who claimed a friend was trapped in a chimney at that very same address.

Kern County firefighters were summoned and freed the burglar, who was covered in ash from head to toe. Taken to jail in nearby Bakersfield, he was charged with burglary, which didn't quite *soot* him.

Honorable Mention: This clumsy burglar literally hampered his own crime when he tried to break into an apartment in Mesa, Arizona, in 2011.

He quietly removed a screen and jumped through an open bedroom window—and fell straight into a clothes hamper. The hamper, which was made of plastic pipes and netting, collapsed on him, trapping him on the floor. The more he struggled to get out of it, the more entangled he became. Any thoughts of burglarizing the place were replaced by worries of how to escape from this dilemma.

The tenant, who was in the bathroom when the hapless intruder gained entry, heard strange noises coming from his bedroom. Seeing the netted crook, the tenant grabbed a broom and restrained him before calling 911. Police arrested the intruder and booked him on charges of burglary and criminal damage. He had fallen into a trap of his own making.

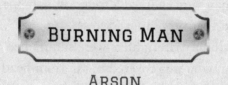

BURNING MAN

ARSON

So this guy goes sneaking around his apartment complex at 3:00 a.m., siphoning gas from neighbors' cars and putting the stolen fuel into his own vehicle. He thinks he's pretty smart and decides to treat himself to a cigarette, which is anything but clever.

He lights up. Sure enough, the gas fumes from his criminal activity erupt into a costly blaze.

According to authorities in Hayward, California, in 2013, this thirty-nine-year-old dunderhead was in the carport area of the Valienzi Manor Apartments, filling his car's fuel tank with gas that he was draining from residents' vehicles. Taking a break, he leaned against his car and flicked a lighter for his cigarette. The spark from the lighter lit the gas vapors in the air, igniting a fire that engulfed the carport and several cars that were parked in it.

The dunce was able to pull his vehicle out before it caught fire, but several neighbors weren't so lucky,

Hayward Fire Department spokesman LaShon Earnest told EastBayTimes.com. The fire damaged two vehicles and destroyed six others worth a total of two hundred thousand dollars. One resident managed to drive her month-old car out of the carport, but not before flames had blistered the roof of the vehicle.

Fortunately, the fire did not spread to the nearby apartment building and nobody was injured. Well, that's not entirely true. One person was injured—the guy who caused all the trouble. The flames didn't hurt him, but a fist did. The fist belonged to a neighbor who, after learning how the fire started, punched Mr. Burning Man in the face.

After the culprit was treated for a black eye, he was booked in Hayward Jail on arson charges and held on seventy-five thousand dollars' bail. So what started as a petty crime turned into a major felony all because of a cigarette, which proves once again that smoking is bad for you.

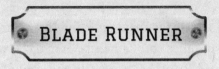

BLADE RUNNER

THEFT

It's common for shoplifters to stuff stolen items down their pants. This petty thief did just that with hunting knives—and discovered they were far sharper than he was.

In 2008, this nutbar walked into a Meijer superstore in Grand Rapids, Michigan, and, when he thought nobody was looking, slid several hunting knives worth three hundred dollars into his waistband, police told WZZM-TV. But somebody was watching, and as the shoplifter headed toward the front of the store, two Meijer security staffers confronted him.

Rather than admit he took the knives, the twenty-six-year-old thief tried to rush past the employees, but they blocked him. During the scuffle that followed, he fell to the floor—and that's when he learned how foolish and painful it was to hide cutlery in his pants. One of the blades stabbed him more than once in the stomach.

He was taken to the hospital, where he was treated for several puncture wounds and then released to the custody of police, who booked him on a misdemeanor shoplifting charge.

Too bad the knife wasn't as dull as his brain.

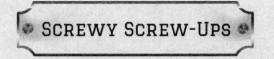

Screwy Screw-Ups

Attempted Assault

These two dumbbells foiled their own attempt to hold up a pharmacy when one accidentally squirted himself in the face with pepper spray while the other unintentionally cut himself with a knife.

One of the dolts strode into a drugstore in the Perth, Australia, suburb of Shoalwater in 2016 and tried to shoplift several items. When the pharmacist spotted him, the perp dashed out the door. But the pharmacist caught up with him in the parking lot, and the two began to fight.

The thief then whipped out a canister of pepper spray, planning to temporarily disable the pharmacist. But the idiot didn't realize the canister was pointing the wrong way. When he tried to spray the pharmacist, the doofus sprayed himself right in the face.

Suddenly, an accomplice appeared and tried to come to the aid of his fellow wrongdoer. Hoping to threaten the pharmacist, the assailant whipped out a sharp knife. But he was careless and sliced his own hand. The bleeding thug and the blinded thief stumbled off into the darkness—victims of their own stupidity.

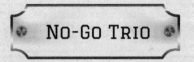

NO-GO TRIO

ATTEMPTED BURGLARY

These three oafs tried to pull off a lucrative heist but were betrayed by their accomplice—a donkey.

In the middle of the night in 2013, the trio stole a ten-year-old donkey named Xavi in the Colombian town of Juan de Acosta, according to *Noticias Caracol*. They planned to use the donkey to carry away all the goods they planned to steal during a burglary of a grocery store.

They entered the store through the roof. Then they loaded up Xavi with bottles of rum, containers of oil, bags of rice, and cans of sardines. They were still adding more pilfered items onto his back when the donkey turned on them and let out a series of loud hee-haws— so loud, in fact, that his braying alerted police at their headquarters nearby. The trio had no choice but to flee, leaving their loot and their honky donkey behind.

THE "CLUES BLUES"

★ BADGES ★

For carelessly leaving an obvious trail of evidence, the Dumb Crooks Hall of Shame inducts the following:

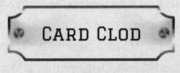

CARD CLOD

BANK ROBBERY

Usually bank robbers try to conceal their identity. But not this Hall of Shamer. Before robbing a bank, he foolishly inserted his ATM debit card at the teller window, forgetting that the card provides all sorts of interesting data—like his name and other personal information.

Oh, if only all crooks left such telltale clues for police. It would make law enforcement officers' jobs so much easier.

According to federal authorities, the fifty-six-year-old dunce was dressed in a checkered double-breasted sport coat when he walked into a branch of Wells Fargo Bank in downtown San Diego in 2016. He went up to a teller window and swiped his card through the card reader at the window. After the teller greeted him, the crook said, "You're being robbed. Don't make a mistake." He then handed the teller a note repeating what he had just said.

When the teller hesitated, the robber said, "You don't want anyone to get hurt. Don't make a mistake."

The teller then handed him 565 dollars in twenties and ones. Clutching the cash, he ran out of the bank. When police arrived and began their investigation, they were delighted to learn that the chucklehead had used his debit card at the teller window. By accessing the data, they learned the culprit's name, address, driver's license number, and criminal background.

FBI agents and San Diego police officers staked out his residence, a nearby hostel. When he left the building, they stopped him and asked him several questions, which he answered. He also let the cops search his room. Authorities found a checkered double-breasted jacket that matched the one the robber wore, as well as his debit card. Knowing that he couldn't talk his way out of the mess he had created, the dork confessed to robbing the bank.

Months later, a judge sentenced him to three years and ten months in prison for the robbery, according to the US Attorney's Office. As part of his sentence, he was ordered to pay 565 dollars in restitution to the bank. It's unlikely he paid it with his debit card.

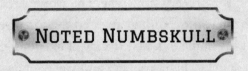

NOTED NUMBSKULL

BANK ROBBERY

This scatterbrain had trouble with spelling and grammar when he handed a note to a teller at the Fifth Third Bank in Chicago in 2008. It said, "Be Quick Be Quit. Give your cash or I'll shoot."

Okay, so he would flunk English 101. But even more telling about his intelligence (or, more accurately, lack of it) was what he wrote the note on.

Minutes before the robbery, he decided to write a demand note instead of verbally threatening the teller. Not having any stationery handy, he pulled out his pay stub from work, ripped it in two, and scribbled on the back of one of the torn halves. The note did its job for the robber and, ultimately, for the FBI.

He handed the note to the teller, who gave him nearly four hundred dollars in cash (which would have been a paltry sum to professional bank robbers). He took the money and ran. In his hurry, he dropped the other half of the torn pay stub. When investigators found it outside the bank doors, it matched perfectly with the other half that had been given to the teller. The best part from law enforcement's point of view was that the front of the torn pay stub revealed the perp's name and the grocery store where he worked. By the end of the day, the FBI had arrested the forty-year-old robber at his home in Cary, Illinois. He later pleaded guilty in court to bank robbery and was sentenced to forty-six months in federal prison.

"It's fairly unusual that we see something that specifically stupid," FBI spokesman Ross Rice told the *Chicago Tribune.*

Rice said most bank robbers aren't masterminds—something many of the stories in this book show. "We had a robber who wrote a demand on a deposit slip with his name on it and another who wrote on the back of an envelope that had his address on the other side," Rice told the *Arlington Daily Herald.* "He's not the first to do this and probably won't be the last."

Hey, all you bad guys, make a note of that!

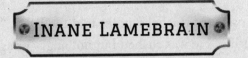

INANE LAMEBRAIN

ATTEMPTED BANK ROBBERY

This half-wit walked into a Welsh bank and tried to rob it. But he left empty-handed because he was empty-headed. He had forgotten that just thirty minutes earlier, he had given the teller his name and address, which was why he was quickly arrested.

The twenty-seven-year-old amateur from Treorchy, South Wales, United Kingdom, had gone to a branch of Barclays Bank in 2014, where he filled out a change-of-address card. When he handed it to teller Catherine Stockton, he was surprised to see that her drawer was full of money. Why he was amazed that a bank teller would have money in a drawer, who knows. But he decided he would come back and relieve her of that cash.

A half hour later, he returned wearing a hoodie and sunglasses—and socks *over* his shoes. How those socks were supposed to help disguise him is anybody's guess. He went over to Stockton, who recognized him from his earlier visit. Unlike when he handed her his change-of-address card, he scowled and flashed a weapon.

"She could see he was holding a bread knife across his body as he demanded all the cash to be handed over," prosecutor Rachel Knight told the BBC. "He was not shouting. He was rushed but not angry or agitated. Ms. Stockton raised the alarm by pressing the panic button."

When the teller refused to hand over the money, the crook left. But if he thought he would get away scot-free, he was wrong. Knowing his name and address, police easily captured him and charged him with attempted bank robbery.

After being found guilty in Crown Court, he was sentenced to two and a half years in prison. Stephen Jeary, his defense attorney, told the BBC, "He told the police it was stupid and he was very sorry."

Yes, he was a very sorry bank robber.

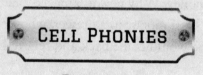

CELL PHONIES

BURGLARY

Sometimes a crook doesn't learn from others' mistakes because he makes them all by himself. Case in point: the sneak who leaves his cell phone behind at the home he has just burglarized. It happened to these two cell *phonies* in separate incidents.

Case No. 1: Like some sort of technological security blanket, this nineteen-year-old from Lake Worth, Florida, felt compelled to bring his cell phone with him when he broke into a house while the owners, a husband and wife, were gone in 2013.

Slinking around the kitchen with an accomplice, the young man took out his cell phone and put it on the counter. Later, after the pair collected jewelry and a shotgun, the burglar grabbed what he assumed was his cell phone. It wasn't. The phone belonged to one of the victims. The noodle head didn't realize that his own phone was still lying on the kitchen counter when he exited the residence.

A short while later, the victims came home and, discovering they had been burglarized, called 911. When deputies from the Palm Beach County Sheriff's Office arrived, the couple pointed to the cell phone and said it wasn't theirs. Everyone wondered, who owned it?

Right on cue, the phone rang and the screen lit up with the name "Mom." An investigator answered the call and talked with the woman on the other end of the line. When he asked her whose phone she had called, she said it belonged to her son and gave his name.

Deputies quickly tracked the perp down. They found the victim's cell phone on him, and forty-nine pieces of the couple's missing jewelry in the purse of his nineteen-year-old accomplice. Both were arrested and faced multiple charges, including burglary and larceny.

Case No. 2: A year later, this forty-six-year-old burglar from Hollywood, Florida, also had phone issues.

He broke into a Hollywood apartment through a bathroom window and stole a flat-screen TV and a coffee table. When the victim returned home, she saw him leaving her apartment. She tried to confront him, but he fled in a pickup.

However, in his haste, the chump accidentally left his cell phone on the victim's bed. Now here's where it gets ridiculous: When he realized his mistake, he called his phone, hoping the victim would somehow, some way find it in her heart to return it to him. After all, it was his. Never mind that the things he stole were hers.

When the jerk called his phone, the person who answered it wasn't the victim, but the police officer who was investigating the burglary. Proving that his smartphone was smarter than he was, the suspect gave the *phone-y* excuse that his phone had been stolen and he needed it back—and then gave his real name to the cop.

The burglar was arrested a short time later. Fingerprints on the phone matched those found at the scene of five other burglaries.

At a court hearing, Broward County judge John "Jay" Hurley, who read the police report, said to the accused, "So, the allegation is you burglarized the home, you left your cell phone, you realized you left your cell phone and then called back, and the police answered the phone, and you told them what your name was over the cell phone. I'm just trying to absorb that."

"Because it was stolen, sir," the defendant explained.

Hurley set the bond at a hundred thousand dollars for the burglary and grand-theft charges linked to the one burglary. Any calls the crook made from jail after that were *from a cell*.

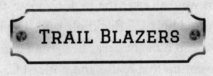

TRAIL BLAZERS

BURGLARY

Cheetos and chips can be unhealthy—especially for these two burglars.

Case No. 1: This nineteen-year-old perp was caught orange-fingered, done in by the crumbs from Cheetos. According to the Kershaw County (South Carolina) Sheriff's Office, about 3:00 a.m. one day in

2013, the goon shattered the front door of the closed Cassatt Country Store in Cassatt. He stole about 160 dollars' worth of beer, cigarettes, snack foods, and energy drinks and caused an estimated 2,500 dollars in damages, store manager Howard "Buck" Buckholz told ABCNews.com.

"In his haste, he punctured two or three bags of Cheetos," the manager said. The dusty orange snack food was strewn over the store's floor and in the doorway. Surveillance video showed that the burglar drove off in a white car. Buckholz said that a neighbor told deputies that a car matching the burglar's vehicle was parked across the street at the Hard Times Café.

"Cheetos were all over the parking lot at the place where he parked his car," Buckholz said. Deputies then began a foot search of the area. Less than a quarter mile away, they went up to a house and noticed Cheetos scattered on the front porch.

After getting permission from the owner of the house to search the residence, deputies encountered the perp, who was staying there as a guest. It was *crunch time* for the suspect. When they went into his room, they found the stolen items. He was taken into custody and charged with second-degree burglary.

Said Buckholz, "He was very easy to catch. It was a very quick deal."

Case No. 2: This intruder gave new meaning to the term "let the chips fall where they may."

The twenty-one-year-old doofus from Washington, Pennsylvania, tried to burglarize the local Subway in the wee hours of the morning in 2012. He shattered three glass windows and a glass door before entering the store. Unfortunately, he cut his hand and foot on the broken glass.

According to the police report, he became frustrated when he discovered that the cash register was locked and "threw cups at the cash register." (How much damage did he think the plastic cups were going to do?) Not wanting to leave empty-handed, he grabbed nine bags of potato chips and fled the scene.

Running while carrying nine slick bags of chips isn't that easy, especially when your hand is bleeding. As he scurried away, the crook kept dropping a bag here and there and didn't bother picking any of them up.

When the cops arrived shortly after the burglary, they spotted a bag of chips outside the Subway and then another several yards away. According to the criminal complaint, "a trail of chips led to the suspect, who was on the steps of Washington High School," which was only a few blocks from the eatery. He wasn't very *chipper* when police arrested him.

Thanks to this dippy drip's chip trip, he was held in the county jail on thirty thousand dollars' bail on charges of burglary, criminal trespass, theft, and criminal mischief. To put it another way, he wasn't the crunchi-est chip in the bag.

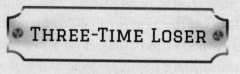

THREE-TIME LOSER

BURGLARY

Judging by his actions, this dingbat's head wasn't too crowded with brains. He left his cell phone at the home he burglarized. But there's more: He also left his car next to the residence because he lost his car keys somewhere in the house. And there's even more: Because he wanted to find his missing phone and keys, he returned to the scene of the crime—while police were there conducting their investigation.

The Twin Falls (Idaho) *Times-News* reported in 2015 that a woman called police to report that when she came home in the afternoon, she found someone had broken into her residence, stolen her jewelry, and ran-sacked the place. The suspect had left cupboards open, scattered books and papers all over the floor, and pried open a file cabinet.

When police arrived, the victim said she found a cell phone on the bed that wasn't hers. And neither was the locked silver 2007 Chevrolet Cobalt parked behind her house.

According to police, while they were continuing their investigation, a woman drove up behind the car and dropped off our Hall of Shamer. When the cops quizzed him, he claimed that a friend had borrowed the car and accidentally locked the keys inside. He said he had arranged for a locksmith to come unlock the car.

No need to wonder if the police believed him. They didn't. Their skepticism was further validated moments later. While the perp was delivering his tall tale to the cops, a resident from the burglarized house came over to them. Dangling a strange set of keys, she said they didn't belong to anyone inside. An officer used a car key from the set to unlock the vehicle and start the engine.

Feigning surprise, the suspect told the police he wasn't the burglar. Yeah, right. Then he claimed he knew the identity of the culprit. Of course he did— because he was the culprit. Officers arrested him on the spot. When they patted him down, they found in his pocket a piece of jewelry belonging to the homeowner.

The cops suspected he was involved in two other burglaries in the neighborhood. At a house nearby, an intruder had broken a window to gain entry, ransacked the place, and stolen jewelry. Footprints found near the garage and the back door matched the shoes that the suspect in custody was wearing, according to police. A few blocks away, a burglar had taken bags of change, checks, and a credit card, which—and this might shock you—were found in the suspect's car.

Upon further questioning at the police station, the twenty-two-year-old crook confessed he was involved in all three break-ins—as if the police had any doubt. He was booked on two charges of burglary and one charge of grand theft.

With all the clues he left behind, he was clueless about how to avoid leaving clues.

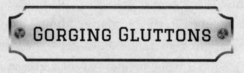

⊛ GORGING GLUTTONS ⊛

BURGLARY

These three burglars ate on the run—literally—and wound up with a bellyache of trouble.

While fleeing from a restaurant they had broken into, the trio took turns eating from a huge stolen bowl of macaroni salad. It was so good they couldn't stop gorging themselves. But the more they ate, the more the addlebrained foodies unwittingly left a trail of the side dish for police to follow.

The culprits broke into the Build-A-Burger restaurant in Mount Morris, New York, during the night in 2015 and dismantled the surveillance system. They tried to open the cash register but didn't know how. The crooks were about as smart as celery stalks because all they had to do was simply turn the key that the owner had left in the register's keyhole.

They decided to haul off the heavy cash register and the surveillance system. But before they left, they wanted to get their *just desserts* by breaking out the ice cream. All each wanted was a *fair shake*, but they couldn't figure out how to operate the mixer. They made a mess of the kitchen, which was full of melting ice cream and *water under the fridge*.

Just as they were getting ready to leave, they opened the refrigerator and spotted a metal bowl containing twelve pounds of restaurant owner Deby Hill's to-die-for macaroni salad. The delicious side dish, which she had prepared hours earlier from a secret family recipe, was simply too tempting to ignore. They wanted to eat all of it right here, right now. However, they had run out of time. Besides, there were *too many crooks in the kitchen*.

Straining to carry the cash register, the surveillance equipment, and the bowl of macaroni salad, the thieving threesome made their getaway on foot along a hiking and biking path. But their stomachs ruled their brains. Not willing to wait until they got home to consume the macaroni salad, they took turns eating it during their escape.

As David Andreatta, columnist for the Rochester *Democrat & Chronicle*, wrote, "Like the burglars, I probably would have eaten it during my getaway. Because if you've ever tasted Hill's macaroni salad, you know you don't wait to eat it, even if you're lugging a 35-pound cash register and cameras through the weeds of the Genesee Valley Greenway hiking trail in the middle of the night on the lam. It's that darn good."

But eating macaroni salad on the run while carrying stolen goods proved to be a sloppy endeavor. Some of the noodles from the yummy side dish fell onto the path as the trio fled.

Later that morning, during the investigation, deputies from the Livingston County Sheriff's Office walked along the path and found parts to the cash register and surveillance system, rubber gloves, loose change, and "a steady trail of macaroni salad," according to a sheriff's news release. Following the tasty trail, deputies soon caught up with the culprits, who were charged with third-degree burglary, third-degree criminal mischief, and fourth-degree grand larceny.

"It was just like Hansel and Gretel," Hill told Andreatta. "[The deputies] followed the line of macaroni salad and all the stuff [the burglars] took out of here. They were not smart criminals."

Hill figured the burglary cost her about two thousand dollars' worth of goods, not including the macaroni salad and the lost business she suffered from having to close the restaurant for a day to clean up their mess and fill out police reports and insurance claims.

As for the burglars, Hill said, "At least they went to jail with a full belly."

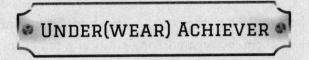

UNDER(WEAR) ACHIEVER

BURGLARY

This crook might have avoided burglary charges if only he had worn different underwear. His undies provided a key clue to his undoing.

The thirty-nine-year-old rogue broke into an occupied home around 6:30 a.m. one day in 2016 in Bridgend, South Wales, United Kingdom. He sneaked into a room that had several cabinets and began rummaging through them, looking for items to steal. While the burglar was bent over, his pants slipped down enough to expose his undies, which weren't your typical boxers. His drawers reflected his love for junk food because they were covered with images of hot dogs, donuts, french fries, and hamburgers.

What skivvies he wore shouldn't have mattered (although you might question his taste in boxers). However, they became his *blunderwear*. While the burglar was squatting by the cabinets during his search for valuables, the owner of the house entered the room and shouted at him. The intruder managed to flee. When police arrived and questioned the homeowner, she described his novelty boxers.

This particular doofus was wanted by the cops for an unrelated matter, so when they spotted him in his car later in the day, they tried to stop him. Determined to elude them, he began driving erratically, forcing officers to dive out of the way as his car scraped the sides of several rock walls that lined the narrow streets. He soon abandoned his vehicle and ran off, but was captured a short time later and brought to jail.

At the time, the police were unaware that he was the same goon who had attempted the morning burglary. But, as the suspect was getting changed into jail clothes, an officer noticed his distinctive boxer shorts, which exactly matched those that the homeowner said the burglar had on. She later made a positive identification of the intruder, who was then charged with burglary.

Detective Constable Darren Bowen told WalesOnline, "The witness in this case and also the officer who recognized the underpants deserve credit because it was their vigilance and attention to detail which no doubt ensured that [the suspect] was linked to the burglary.

"He is a prolific criminal who will spend a number of years behind bars where he belongs. No doubt he'll spend a few of those years thinking about how he should have put his lucky underpants on that day."

BAG MAN

UNARMED ROBBERY

Maybe this loon wasn't born to be a criminal. After all, he left his birth certificate at the scene of a mugging he was accused of committing. Oh, and he also left behind a letter from his mom—one addressed to him.

According to police, in 2013, the twenty-six-year-old suspect was waiting in the dark in Boston's Dorchester neighborhood for a victim to rob. He spotted a woman who had just exited a mass transit stop and followed her to a schoolyard around midnight.

A mugger usually has to have at least one hand free so he can snatch a purse or grab a wallet. But our Hall of Shamer was carrying a bag in each hand. He dropped the bags and then ran up to the victim to snatch her clutch wallet. She put up a fight, but he overpowered her and took off with her wallet, which contained her ID and forty dollars.

In his desire to run off, he forgot two important things—his bags, which he had failed to retrieve. When police arrived, they didn't need to worry about DNA or fingerprints or other evidence concerning the identity of the mugger. He left them with everything they needed. According to the police report, "the bags contained clothes, hygiene products, and a pair of sneakers. Additionally, at the top of one of the bags was a birth certificate that identified [the suspect] as born in 1987, as well as a letter addressed to [the suspect] from his mother."

About an hour later and a block from the scene of the crime, officers stopped a man who fit the victim's description of the robber. The suspect gave them a fake name, but they took it with a *grain of assault*. Officers contacted the victim, who came over and positively identified him as the mugger. Police arrested him on a charge of unarmed robbery and later confirmed his real identity, which matched the name on his birth certificate and the letter from his mother. The mugger had no *bag* of tricks to get out of this mess.

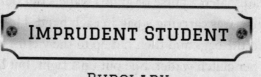

IMPRUDENT STUDENT

BURGLARY

Good crooks do their homework. Bad ones sometimes get done in by their homework. How true that was for this shady high school student who made a really bad choice.

In 2012, the punk entered the unlocked window of a residence in Orem, Utah, at 4:26 a.m., according to the Orem Police Department. The elderly homeowner was awakened by a light in his office. When he went to investigate, he found the intruder rifling through the drawers of a desk. The homeowner confronted the burglar, who then punched him in the face and fled. A check of the residence showed that the only item missing was a camera.

Police sergeant Craig Martinez told reporters that when the cops arrived, they searched inside and outside for clues. They found a good clue in the backyard—a backpack. It didn't have a name on it, but it did have a flash drive. When an officer plugged it into a USB port of a computer, he pulled up the stored homework assignments belonging to a certain eighteen-year-old student.

Martinez said that police went to the student's home and found him asleep on the couch. Near him was the stolen camera, which officers returned to the homeowner. The young crook was arrested and booked into the Utah County Jail on charges related to burglary and theft. Hopefully, he got schooled there about making better choices.

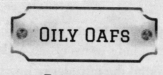

OILY OAFS

BURGLARY

These two not-so-slick crooks literally greased the way for the cops to find them.

In Chickasha, Oklahoma, in 2015, the devious duo kicked in the back door of a residence and stole about four thousand dollars' worth of items, including two TVs, a golf bag and clubs, fishing poles, a camera, and a portable air conditioner. The perps might have succeeded with their crime had they left the Presto deep fryer alone. But, nope, they had to have it. So even though it contained cooking oil, they hauled it off with the other things.

The deep fryer was *greased enlightening* to the police. According to the arrest affidavit, the officer who investigated the burglary "observed noticeable grease spots on the concrete on the back porch," and "grease spots continued west from the [victim's] back door and continued across the road to the backyard gate" of a house less than a block away.

The greasy trail led the cops to the residence of one of the perps, who was a neighbor of the victim. Police told Oklahoma City TV station KFOR that the crook consented to a search of his home, where they found two TVs and two fishing poles under a child's bed, a portable air conditioner in a child's closet, a camera in a baby's crib, and a deep fryer in the utility room.

"It was pretty easy to put two and two together," a neighbor told the TV station. "I saw the trail and could tell what happened."

The arrest affidavit said that the oily pair admitted to the burglary. Although they said they were sorry and returned all the stolen items—including the fryer that led police directly to them—they were still arrested and booked in Grady County Jail.

As for the victim, you couldn't blame her if she was *oiling mad.*

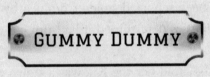

GUMMY DUMMY

GRAND THEFT AUTO

This Hall of Shamer helped police take a bite out of crime—by leaving her dentures in the car that she was accused of stealing.

The Lake County (Florida) Sheriff's Office began receiving reports of a suspicious person snooping around a neighborhood in the town of Lady Lake one night in 2017. When deputies arrived in the area, they spotted a Kia with its door open, overhead interior light on, and key in the ignition. Near the car was the suspect, who was trying to enter a pickup truck.

When they confronted her, deputies saw that she had no teeth and no shoes. Her answers to basic questions didn't seem to make any sense, leading officers to think she was a troubled homeless person.

They had planned to take her to the hospital for a mental evaluation when they looked inside the Kia. Lo and behold, sitting on the front seat were a set of dentures and a pair of pink tennis shoes. Upon further questioning, the suspect, now suddenly acting sane, admitted they were hers. Then the deputies ran a check of the vehicle and discovered something interesting— the car had been reported stolen from nearby Marion County. Deputies determined it had run out of gas in Lady Lake.

When they told her the Kia was a stolen vehicle, the still toothless woman claimed she was only a passenger and that she didn't know who had driven her there. She found out pretty quickly who was going to drive her to her next destination—the deputies. They took her to the Lake County Jail, where she was booked on charges of possession of a stolen vehicle and grand theft auto. There was nothing she could do but grit her teeth—if she had any.

THE "BETTER LUCK NEXT TIME"
★ HONORS ★

*For picking the wrong place, wrong time,
or wrong victim when committing a crime,
the Dumb Crooks Hall of Shame
inducts the following:*

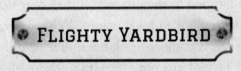

FLIGHTY YARDBIRD

OBSTRUCTING JUSTICE

If you're being chased by the cops, where's the last place you'd hide? Yep, in a prison. But that's exactly where this fleeing troublemaker tried to conceal himself.

It was all so needless. One night in 2010, shortly after 1:00 a.m., the twenty-year-old meathead was driving with friends in the Cleveland suburb of Garfield Heights, Ohio, when police tried to pull him over for a minor traffic violation. Rather than stop and get a ticket (or possibly just a warning), the idiot pressed his foot on the accelerator. The chase was on.

He led police on a wild pursuit through several communities and onto two local interstates, I-480 and I-77, reaching speeds of ninety miles an hour. He squealed off I-77 and zoomed into an industrial area in Cleveland before screeching to a stop.

He and his three passengers bolted from the car. Police apprehended two of them who had blindly run down a dead-end alley. Another guy tried to climb a chain-link fence, but was Tasered by the cops.

The driver, however, did manage to scale the same fence and jumped to the ground on the other side, thinking he had foiled his pursuers. Whatever satisfaction he felt was short-lived, because little did he know that he had just put himself in prison—literally. You see, the fence surrounded a state correctional facility, the Northeast Pre-Release Center for Women. The moment he breached the fence, an alarm went off inside the prison yard, alerting guards who then seized him.

"He ended up in the prison yard," Captain Robert Sackett of the Garfield Heights Police Department told Cleveland TV station WJW. "He was apprehended. He had nowhere to go. It was a little easier to get in than get out."

Police said this chase goes down in history as one of the dumbest moves by a suspect. What makes you want to shake your head is that the driver initially faced only a traffic ticket. But now the yardbird was dealing with several serious charges, including fleeing, and eluding and obstructing justice.

Said Sackett, "They're not all this easy to catch."

Honorable Mention: Two burglary suspects running from the cops turned themselves in at the police station. Not intentionally but stupidly.

During an afternoon in 2016 in Boca Raton, Florida, an alert citizen spotted two men and a woman who had just burglarized a house. The witness called 911, giving a detailed description of the suspects and their getaway car. When officers tried to stop the vehicle, it crashed. The woman surrendered but the two men ran off with the police on their heels.

The pair could have gone in any one of several directions, but they chose to head northwest. Wrong choice. Up ahead was a wooden fence. Had they known what was on the other side, they would have made a U-turn. But they didn't. Without slowing down, they climbed over it and saw they were now in a place they really didn't want to be—the parking lot of the Boca Raton Police Department. This discovery was made all the more obvious by the number of officers who, having been alerted by pursuing cops, had rushed out of the station with their guns pointed at the suspects. The pair and their accomplice were charged with grand theft and burglary. Their offense had been curtailed by *de fence*.

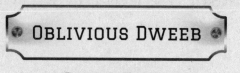

OBLIVIOUS DWEEB

GRAND THEFT

Who would attempt to steal a big flat-screen TV at a store where a Shop-with-a-Cop event is going on at the same time? Well, a really, really dumb crook would, that's who.

During the 2016 holiday season, deputies from the Port St. Lucie (Florida) Sheriff's Office took part in an annual event to help underprivileged children. The deputies picked up the kids at the Williams Center in nearby Fort Pierce and took them to the Walmart store in St. Lucie West. Paired up with a deputy, the children, who otherwise couldn't afford to buy gifts for their parents and siblings, were allowed to pick out clothes, toys, shoes, and other items to give to family members. The purchases were paid for with donations to the cause.

This had always been a big, festive event at the store, and any lawbreaker with even a hint of awareness would know the right time to shoplift a big-ticket item certainly isn't when the place is teeming with cops.

As surveillance cameras showed, the suspect picked up a boxed fifty-eight-inch television, put it in his shopping cart, and casually strolled around the store, which was bustling with holiday shoppers—and deputies. He had a cell phone to his ear as he headed out of the Walmart with the TV, which he didn't pay for.

Just past the checkout lanes, he was confronted by an employee. The birdbrained shoplifter then abandoned the cart, dashed back inside, and tried to escape through another door. He didn't get far, not with all those deputies chasing him. They had him in custody in no time and charged him with grand theft and resisting an officer without violence.

He paid a price for not paying attention.

Honorable Mention: Two thugs strolled to the back of a convenience store to steal snacks and beer. They glanced around to make sure no one was watching them. Did they have blinders on? Did they forget their eyeglasses? Did they not see the four Los Angeles County sheriff's deputies standing at the front of the store? Uh, well, no. No they didn't.

Less than a minute before the stooges had entered the Chevron Food Mart in La Mirada, California, at about 4:00 a.m. in 2011, deputies had parked their two marked patrol vehicles by the side of the store and walked inside. Somehow the dumb duo had failed to spot the squad cars. Once inside, the crooks were so focused on their beer and snack heist that they still didn't notice the uniformed deputies, who were by the cash register.

The unaware pair swiped a case of beer and munchies, totaling about twenty dollars, and sprinted out of the store. Also sprinting out of the store were the four deputies, who promptly seized the thieves and charged them with burglary and petty theft. So much for their beer run.

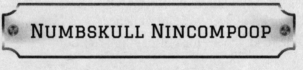

NUMBSKULL NINCOMPOOP

THEFT

This thief tried stealing gas by siphoning it from a tour bus, which was *fuelish* enough. Even worse, he mistakenly sucked on a hose that began draining the sewage tank instead of the fuel tank, making him a true *nincompoop*.

The visiting vehicle was parked overnight in Laverton, Western Australia, in 2016 when the crook sneaked up on it with a hose, intent on emptying the gas tank. The thief planned to use the old tried-and-true siphoning method of sticking the hose in the fuel tank, then sucking on the other end of the hose until the gas started flowing into one of several large cans that he had brought.

Here's where the egghead made a bad blunder: The bus had two separate tanks—one for gas and one for waste from the on-board bathroom. He stuck the hose in what he thought was the gas tank but was actually the sewage tank. Then he began sucking on the hose. Imagine the revolting surprise the perp got when the first stream of waste reached his mouth. At that point, the thief lost his appetite for crime (or anything else, for that matter).

The next morning the bus driver found the cap to the waste tank on the ground. The fuel tank cap was still on securely and none of the fuel had been stolen.

"We can infer he beat a very hasty retreat, with a somewhat bitter taste in his mouth," Senior Sergeant Heath Soutar of the Laverton Police Department told the *West Australian*.

He said that while the cops were looking for the offender, they "have absolutely zero interest" in tracking down any of the stolen poop. If they did, they could call it The Case of the *Stool* Bus.

Honorable Mention: A mugger in Santa Cruz, California, hoped he had made off with a bag of money. But his effort was a total *waste*.

The nitwit, a man in his twenties, approached a sixty-two-year-old woman as she was walking her dog one morning in 2011. According to the *Santa Cruz Sentinel*, he demanded the woman give him everything she had, and if she refused, he would kick her dog. The woman handed over the only thing she had on her—the small plastic bag that she was holding. Hoping it contained something of value, the mugger snatched it and ran off.

You guessed it: This yahoo had swiped a bag of dog poop!

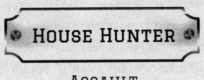

❖ HOUSE HUNTER ❖

ASSAULT

This heedless teenager was running from police, desperately trying to find somewhere to hide in a residential neighborhood. He finally found a house. But of all the possibilities, he couldn't have picked a worse one.

The punk was fleeing the cops after assaulting his foster mother in the Miami suburb of Opa Locka, Florida, in 2013. Hopping over fences, plowing through bushes, and sprinting between garages, he had managed to dodge police. But on this hot, sunny day, the chase was wearing him down. He needed somewhere to hide. Then he spotted a man standing in the front yard of a residence.

"[The teenager] stopped, put his hands on his legs, trying to catch his breath," the homeowner later recalled for Miami TV station WTVJ. "He says, 'I'm running from the police. Can you help me?' I said, 'Sure I can help you.'"

According to the TV report, the teen walked into the home of this friendly man and plopped down on a leather couch. Relieved that he had found a sanctuary, he took off his shirt and wiped the sweat off his face. He failed to pay any attention to his surroundings. If he had, he would have noticed the many photos on the wall of the homeowner—in a police uniform—and spotted the police radio on the table.

Had he been more aware, he also would have overheard the homeowner on the phone talking in cop jargon to someone at the Miami-Dade Police Department.

A few minutes later, the teen looked out the window and saw patrol cars pulling up to the house. He turned to the homeowner and asked, "What are we going to do?"

"I don't know what *we're* going to do, but *you're* going to jail," the man told him before opening the door. Police came in, handcuffed the teen, and took him to the Department of Juvenile Justice, where he was held on a charge of aggravated battery.

Of all the houses in the area, the kid had sought refuge in the one residence he should have avoided the most—the one belonging to a detective for Miami-Dade County Public Schools.

Honorable Mention: A felon who was being chased by the cops played the odds just as badly as the teenager in Opa Locka.

Having just burglarized a house in Lighthouse Point, Florida, in 2014, the outlaw hopped in a car that had been reported stolen. License-plate recognition cameras detected the vehicle and alerted police, who soon spotted the perp driving the car. When they attempted to stop him, he drove through a chain-link fence in a wild effort to elude them.

He led the cops on a high-speed chase onto busy I-95 before he abandoned the car. He then dashed across the ten-lane expressway like in the old Frogger video game, as vehicles whizzed past him or swerved to avoid hitting him. When he reached the other side, he was unable to scale the high wall, so he sprinted back across all the lanes of traffic while deputies from the Broward County Sheriff's Office were pursuing him on foot and in squad cars.

He jumped over a chain-link fence and ran into a neighborhood, looking for someone to help him. While on a side street, he flagged down the next car that came by. The plain-looking vehicle stopped, and when the fugitive asked for a ride, the driver was happy to oblige. The driver gave the culprit a ride—straight to jail, where he was charged with burglary, speeding, driving with a suspended license, resisting arrest, and reckless driving.

You see, the man behind the wheel was an undercover sheriff's deputy.

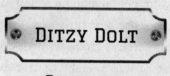

DITZY DOLT

BURGLARY

Any good burglar ("good" meaning at his or her illegal craft, not as a person) would case out the place before attempting a break-in. Not so for this Hall of Shamer. He walked right in on the cops.

The forty-nine-year-old bumbler was a hopeless burglar. But give him props for persistence because he had been found guilty a whopping thirty-six times on various burglary charges. And still he kept trying. He was clearly a man who *stood by his convictions*.

In keeping with his incompetence, he tried to break into a house in Abington, England, one night in 2013 and failed miserably. While attempting to gain entry, he cut himself on the door lock and walked away, leaving behind a trail of blood.

Still looking to pull off a burglary that night in the same neighborhood, he noticed the window on the back door of another house was already broken. This looked like a made-to-order entry for the burglar. No need to check the place out first to see if someone might be home. Why bother?

Well, here's why: The house had already been burglarized earlier that night by someone else, and two police officers were now inside interviewing the victim. That's probably not the best time or place to attempt a burglary. But our careless crook wasn't aware of the cops' presence because he was too lazy to case the house first.

So, moments after he slipped his hand through the broken back-door window and unlocked the handle, he crept inside. Oh, was he in for a surprise. Startled by the two cops, he tried to flee, but was promptly apprehended.

Described by his own attorney as "clumsy" and "pathetic," the culprit was found guilty of the break-ins. Sentencing the burglar to twenty-four months of community service and mandatory participation in a program for repeat offenders, Judge Rupert Mayo told him, "You virtually fell into the hands of the police officer. You are not a very good burglar. Were there any sense of professionalism, I would not be giving you the chance I am giving you."

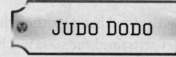

JUDO DODO

CARJACKING

This bonehead picked the wrong vehicle to carjack. It was packed with members of a judo club. Man, did he flip out.

One afternoon in 2002 in Los Angeles, the twenty-year-old bubblehead approached a couple in their car. He pulled the man out of the vehicle, got into the driver's seat, and sped off with the woman still inside. A few blocks away, he stopped and grabbed her purse. During the struggle, he shoved her out of the car and then drove to a nearby gas station, where he got out hoping to carjack another vehicle.

Hey, that beige minivan looks like easy pickings, he thought. *Probably belongs to a soccer mom.* Oh, appearances can be deceiving. The vehicle was a rental full of members of the coed judo club from Florida International University. The students, who had been in town to teach classes in nearby Long Beach, had stopped at the gas station on their way to Los Angeles International Airport for their flight home.

The hooligan approached one of the female judo experts, who was standing outside the minivan, and tried to shove her out of the way. Within seconds, she had him on the ground while her teammates poured out of the minivan and assisted her by putting their skills into practice. They restrained the goon in a body hold while waiting for the police to arrive. "We had this guy like a pretzel on the ground," Nestor Bustillo, the club's judo instructor, told the *Los Angeles Times*.

Yep, the crook was *thrown for a loss*.

LAPD sergeant Alan Hamilton of the Hollywood Division told the newspaper that when the judo club members forced the carjacker into submission, he was bloodied up by the time police arrived. He was treated at the scene and transported to jail, where he faced multiple charges, including carjacking, kidnapping, and mugging.

"He was detained, to say the least," Hamilton said. "Judo team, one; carjacker, zero."

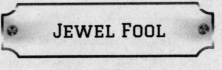

JEWEL FOOL

GRAND THEFT

Sometimes fate just loves to have fun at the expense of bad crooks. This simpleton unknowingly tried to sell stolen jewelry at a shop managed by the very person whose house he had just burglarized.

The thirty-three-year-old crook had broken into a residence in Immokalee, Florida, one afternoon in 2011 and scooped up thousands of dollars' worth of jewelry. Hoping to make some quick cash, he planned to sell the valuables to a store. He had plenty of places to choose from, including shops in nearby Fort Myers and Naples, but he decided on Marilyn's Boutique in downtown Immokalee.

When the perp walked into the store, he received a friendly greeting from the manager. Telling her he had several nice pieces of used jewelry that he wished to sell, he laid them out on the counter. As she looked them over, she thought the jewelry was indeed quite nice, quite expensive—and quite recognizable. They were all identical to the pieces she kept at home.

Even though she was unaware that he had burglarized her house, she was growing increasingly suspicious. She excused herself for a moment and went to the back of the shop, where she phoned her husband at his workplace. He said he would call 911 and meet her at the shop. Remaining calm, she returned to the customer and kept him engaged in conversation until her husband and Collier County sheriff's deputies arrived simultaneously.

While the thief was taken to the sheriff's substation in Immokalee for further questioning, deputies accompanied the store manager's husband to their house, where they found the back door had been forced open. The inside of the residence had been ransacked—and the woman's jewelry was missing.

The perp was arrested on charges of grand theft and dealing in stolen property. Meanwhile, fate had a belly laugh.

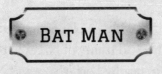

BAT MAN

ROBBERY

This lamebrain decided to rob a gun shop during business hours using his baseball bat as his only weapon. What he failed to consider was that the employees in the gun shop were gun enthusiasts who took their Second Amendment rights seriously—and had licenses to carry concealed weapons.

Ignoring the reality that wielding a baseball bat in a store full of gun-carrying workers is foolhardy at best, our Hall of Shamer barged into Discount Gun Sales in Beaverton, Oregon, one afternoon in 2013 and smashed a display counter with his bat. But as the hooligan was grabbing for one of the unloaded guns, the store manager simply pulled out his own personal—and fully loaded—firearm and pointed it at the would-be robber. *Hey, batter! You're out!*

The manager ordered the batter to drop to the floor. The smartest thing the dumb crook did was comply with the manager's command. When the police arrived, the culprit was still on the floor at gunpoint. He was arrested on, among other charges, first-degree robbery and theft.

Wrote *Slate* correspondent Justin Peters, "As everyone who's ever played rock-gun-baseball bat knows, gun always beats baseball bat . . . It's generally not a good idea to try to rob a gun shop, unless you are in a tank, or are yourself some sort of bulletproof robot. [He] could've made things easier on himself by picking an easier target, like a Jo-Ann Fabrics or the Good Ship Lollipop."

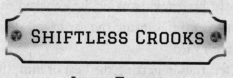

SHIFTLESS CROOKS

AUTO THEFT

Man, if you're going to steal a car, at least make sure you know how to operate one. In separate roll-your-eyes incidents, these shiftless crooks got nabbed because they targeted vehicles with manual transmissions, which they had no clue how to drive.

Case No. 1: In Omaha, Nebraska, in 2014, this seventeen-year-old boy was armed with a plastic Airsoft gun when he tried to carjack a Dodge Caliber hatchback. After forcing a mother and her son out of the car, which was parked in their driveway, the scofflaw jumped into the vehicle. But now he had a problem. The Caliber didn't have an automatic transmission. It had a stick shift—something totally unfamiliar to him.

As the victims watched from their house—after they called 911—the culprit spent the next seven minutes unsuccessfully trying to put the car in gear. He jammed on the clutch, jerked the gear selector, pushed buttons, and twisted knobs. Nothing worked, although he unwittingly switched on the windshield wipers and the lights. In his growing panic, he knocked the gear selector into neutral, causing the car to roll slowly onto the neighbor's yard.

With frustration getting the best of him, the ditz leaped out of the vehicle just as police cruisers rolled up. A brief foot chase ended in his capture and arrest. He eventually pleaded guilty to the carjacking as well as armed robbery at three stores—where he stole video games—and was sentenced in Douglas County District Court to eight to fourteen years in prison.

"For those of you who still have stick shift vehicles, there is an advantage today," Lieutenant Mike McGee told WOWT-TV. "Young people don't know how to drive them."

Case No. 2: These three teens tried to steal a woman's car in Seattle in 2014, but suffered an epic fail because they couldn't operate a manual transmission.

A seventy-year-old woman was getting something out of the trunk of her Kia when the trio approached her. At gunpoint, she gave up the keys to her car and stepped away. Then she watched in bemusement as they struggled over how to work the stick shift.

"I got a five speed in there," the victim later told TV station KIRO. "They couldn't figure out how to get it going."

Unable to drive away, the exasperated threesome ran across the street and disappeared.

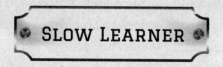

SLOW LEARNER

ATTEMPTED BANK ROBBERY

Attempting to rob a bank, a career criminal stormed into the building and then stopped dead in his tracks. Where were the tellers? Where were the security guards? Where were the customers?

There were none for good reason. It was no longer a bank. In fact, it hadn't been a bank in seventeen years!

With twenty-two convictions over a forty-year period, the fifty-seven-year-old nitwit never figured out that perhaps he wasn't cut out for a life of crime because he was so bad at it. His ill-fated attempt at a felony confirmed he was an inept miscreant.

In 2011, he was determined to rob what he thought was the branch of a bank in Osnabrück, Germany.

Armed with a toy pistol, he stole a car and drove it into the city, where he parked it outside the building. Waving the "gun," he ran inside, grabbed a passerby, and, using her as a hostage, demanded more than ten thousand euros (about thirteen thousand dollars) from the bank employees. Except there weren't any bank employees. Only then did he discover he was standing in the lobby not of a bank but a physical therapy center. Had he been paying attention during the previous two decades, he would have known that way back in 1994 the bank had moved out of the building, which was then converted into the health facility.

What to do? What to do? Seeing an ATM in the lobby, the chowderhead forced his hostage at gunpoint to withdraw more than five hundred euros from the machine. After stuffing the cash in his pocket, the robber dashed out of the building, jumped into the stolen car, and drove off. He abandoned the vehicle a short while later, but left his toy gun, which was covered with his fingerprints, on the seat.

Because he had such an extensive criminal record, the police quickly found a fingerprint match. Knowing the identity of the culprit, the cops arrested him in no time. He later pleaded guilty and was sentenced to seven years in prison in one of the most poorly timed robberies ever committed. At least behind bars, this sad character could have a *wail of a time.*

THE "GOTCHA"
★ CITATIONS ★

For getting caught in the act because of a ridiculous blunder, the Dumb Crooks Hall of Shame inducts the following:

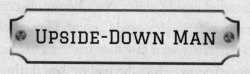

❖ UPSIDE-DOWN MAN ❖

BURGLARY

This seasoned burglar found his criminal life turned topsy-turvy when he tried to break into a house. He got his foot stuck in a window, which left him hanging upside down for more than an hour. Even worse, while he was dangling in plain view, neighbors and passersby gathered to jeer him.

According to authorities, the thirty-two-year-old chucklehead from Dartford, Kent, England, was walking past a Victorian terrace home in the early evening in 2008 when he noticed a transom window was slightly open. He thought this would be an easy residence to burglarize even though it was still daylight. He knocked on the front door to determine if anybody was inside. No one answered, so he climbed onto the exterior windowsill and opened the transom window, which was chest-high and directly above a larger plate-glass window.

Slipping through the transom window headfirst, the intruder curled his body over the top of the lower window and slid facedown toward the floor until . . . misfortune. The transom window unexpectedly slammed shut on his left foot, trapping him and leaving him suspended upside down. No amount of wriggling could free him from this predicament. He was clearly visible to passersby who saw him through the larger plate-glass window, which he had broken during his struggle to get loose.

If that wasn't humiliating enough, our Hall of Shamer was subjected to the further indignity of cat-calls from a growing crowd attracted by the odd sight of a squirming man suspended upside down by his foot that was caught in a window. According to the *Daily Mail*, about thirty people showed up over the next hour and ridiculed him. Speaking through his shirt, which had flopped over his head, he pleaded for help. But no one offered to assist him. And, apparently, no one was in any hurry to call the police.

Then the homeowner, Paul Ives, showed up. "[The robber] was screaming to get him down, and we were all saying, 'I don't think so,'" Ives told the newspaper. Still twisting in the air, the blundering bozo claimed that he had spotted burglars trying to break into the house and he had selflessly attempted to catch the scoundrels only to end up stuck like this.

Ives told the *Daily Mail*, "He kept saying, 'I haven't done anything. I was stopping the burglars.'" No one believed a word of the hapless intruder's cockamamy story.

Shortly after someone called authorities, paramedics released his foot from the transom window. He was free, but only for a few seconds before police handcuffed him and spirited him off to jail.

Although he was suspected in dozens of other break-ins, the crook pleaded guilty in court to one count of burglary and was sentenced to three years in prison. His defense attorney, Mark Dacey, admitted to the BBC, "It was a pathetic burglary. It's clear he was subjected to some public humiliation."

He will probably have a *hang-up* over this for years to come.

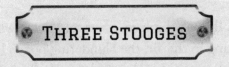

THREE STOOGES

BURGLARY

This trio of amateur thieves failed miserably when two of them broke into a bank and discovered too late that their master plan and their backup plan wouldn't work. Adding to their ineptness, the pair tripped the alarm. And what was the third guy—who was the driver of the getaway car and the lookout—doing all this time? He was asleep at the wheel.

According to Miami-Dade (Florida) police, the threesome—all in their twenties—drove to a branch of Wachovia Bank in South Beach at 5:45 a.m. one Sunday in 2010. Two got out and broke the front window to gain entry to the closed bank. Meanwhile, in the car, the lookout took a nap.

Inside the bank, the pair discovered their ill-conceived plan was, well, ill-conceived. They had assumed the bank kept cash in the tellers' drawers. Their assumption was wrong. When the bank closed for the night, all the bills were stored in a locked vault. Not having the skill or high-tech gear to break it open, the dingbat duo went to plan B. They began gathering all the nickels, dimes, and quarters they could find in the tellers' drawers and hauling them in bags to the front of the bank.

What about the lookout? He was still snoozing in the car.

Instead of the quick-hit, in-and-out bank job that the trio had originally plotted, the backup plan took much longer than they had anticipated. Did you know that bags filled with hundreds of coins are heavy? Yeah, well, they didn't discover that interesting tidbit until they had cleaned out the drawers of change and begun lugging the bags across the floor.

Then came their next mistake. When they opened the door shortly before 7:00 a.m., they carelessly tripped the silent alarm. Before they could haul the bags out of the bank, they heard police cars arriving. There was no way the two burglars could run off with all that bounty weighing them down, so they tried to hide in the bank.

And what was their pal doing through all of this? He was still dozing in the car. Boy, did he have a *rude awakening*! The cops roused him from dreamland and arrested him on the spot.

After learning from the lookout that his fellow crooks were still in the bank, officers convinced one of them to come out and surrender. But the other one had scampered to the bank's second floor and was hiding above the ceiling tiles. Police dogs located him, but he still wouldn't come down from his hiding place—that is, not until the ceiling gave way and he crashed to the floor in front of the cops. His *fall from grace* ended with his arrest.

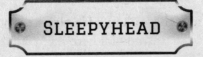

SLEEPYHEAD

BURGLARY

This Hall of Shamer was living proof of the expression, "If you snooze, you lose."

According to the Sarasota County (Florida) Sheriff's Office, the twenty-nine-year-old loon from Nokomis, Florida, broke into a residence while the homeowner, Bob Wotring, was gone one night in 2014. The burglar went through the house gathering jewelry and other valuables. It looked like this would be an extremely profitable score.

But this life of crime had its downside. It was taxing and stressful, so he decided to take a catnap. He flopped down on the edge of the owner's bed and closed his eyes. And he slept and he slept, and his slumber lumbered on for several hours into the morning.

While the intruder was deep in sleep, Wotring's housekeeper arrived and noticed something unsettling as she walked through the home. Wotring later told Sarasota TV station WWSB that his jewelry "was all sitting neatly in piles" and silverware had been pulled out of kitchen drawers. Wotring said that the burglar had gone through the entire house making mounds of valuables to steal. "All these drawers were pulled and open with stuff hanging out," the homeowner said.

The housekeeper received the shock of her life after stepping into the bedroom. There was a strange man at the end of the bed, sound asleep on his back, with a clear plastic bag crammed with jewelry by his side. The housekeeper immediately phoned 911 and told the dispatcher that the suspected burglar was in the home asleep.

Sheriff's deputies arrived quickly and quietly. "They were wonderful about coming here without sirens to wake him up, and they did a perfect job," Wotring told the TV station. Even when deputies entered the room, the burglar was still snoozing.

Before waking him up, deputies took photos of him asleep on the bed and then posted a picture on the sheriff's office's Facebook page, which said, "Talk about falling asleep on the job!!! A cleaning lady called deputies Monday morning when she found [the suspect] inside her client's Nokomis home. He was passed out with a bag full of stolen jewelry next to him on the bed and didn't even notice the deputies taking pictures! #FloriDUH." The photo went viral.

After deputies woke him up, they charged him with burglary of an unoccupied dwelling and took him to Sarasota County Jail in lieu of a ten-thousand-dollar bond. There was no word on whether or not he *lost sleep over* his arrest.

MASQUERADE RENEGADE

BANK ROBBERY

This bank robber had one of the goofiest disguises ever—multicolored clown pants and a woman's blond wig. If he was trying to convince bank employees he was a woman, he should have shaved off his thick black beard and mustache.

His wacky getup led to a crazy letdown for him.

In 2010 in Swissvale, Pennsylvania, the forty-eight-year-old nutbar shoplifted a BB gun from a local Kmart, and then walked into a branch of Citizens Bank a few blocks away. Pointing the unloaded weapon at a teller, he passed her a note that read, "This is a hold up. Do not put no dye packs in no money because I will see your family and also your kids."

After she gave him an undisclosed amount of cash in a big envelope, he fled. Because he was dressed like a buffoon that would draw attention from any passerby, you would think he would want to immediately ditch the costume to look like a normal person. Not so for this noodle head.

As video from a security camera showed, the robber was still in his zany disguise when he hid behind a tree near the bank and opened the envelope to see how much cash he had stolen. Then he dropped it when the dye pack exploded, turning his hands and the money bright red.

He picked up the cash and ran to a nearby gas station, where he asked motorists for a lift. Yeah, like they were going to give a ride to a bearded guy in clown pants, a wig, and red-dyed hands holding red-dyed money. When they all refused, he jumped into a woman's car. She bailed immediately, but smartly took her keys. While running away, she called 911 on her cell phone.

Officers who were on their way to the bank to investigate the robbery detoured straight to the gas station, where they arrested the perp, who, bewilderingly, had remained in the woman's car. He was arrested and held in jail on 230,000 dollars' bail.

Swissvale police chief Greg Geppert told Pittsburgh TV station KDKA, "He would get my nomination for dumbest criminal. I mean, with a blondish wig, he still has his black facial hair. Definitely different."

Apparently, the robber liked his beard and mustache; they had *grown on him.*

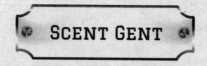

SCENT GENT

RECKLESS DRIVING

This rogue applied far too much cologne to his body in the hopes it might attract the ladies. Instead, it attracted the cops.

He was driving in his hometown of Lebanon, Oregon, in the wee hours of the morning in 2014 when an officer tried to stop him for speeding and going through a red light. Rather than take his medicine, he tried to outrun the cop, triggering a high-speed chase that reached more than a hundred miles an hour and involved several squad cars. The driver was going so fast that the wind resistance ripped off the hood of his Honda Prelude.

When police called off the dangerous pursuit, the scofflaw drove into a neighborhood and abandoned his car. But the cops spotted it a short time later. Witnesses said they had seen a lone man running away from the vehicle, so police began a foot search.

They didn't have to go far. Although it was dark outside and the foliage was dense, they knew he was close. That's because they could smell him. The over-powering scent from his cologne led police right to the dummy, who was hiding behind a bush.

He was booked into the Linn County Jail on several

charges, including felony attempt to elude and reckless driving. When the cops explained how easy he made it for them to locate him, he told them he regretted applying so much cologne. Now that he was behind bars, he had an *in-scent-ive* to give up crime.

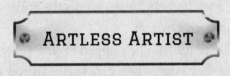

ARTLESS ARTIST

CRIMINAL MISCHIEF

Graffiti has its place, but it sure isn't on the side of police cars. This rascal knew that, but during one unwise spur-of-the-moment decision, he did it anyway.

During an afternoon in 2015, he was painting outside his home when two cruisers from the Gulfport (Florida) Police Department pulled up and parked in front of his residence. The officers stepped out and went to a neighbor's house. For some unfathomable reason, our Hall of Shamer was upset that the cops had the audacity to park on a public street in front of his home.

He chose to express his annoyance in an artistic— yet clearly illegal—way. With a can of blue paint in one hand and a brush in the other, he stomped over to the police cruisers. As you know, you should never deface anyone's vehicle, let alone two squad cars. But he was too angry to stop himself and instead let creativity be his guide. Unfortunately, creativity guided him into vandalism.

As the forty-four-year-old scoundrel tried to explain later to Bay News 9, "I was full of stuff and vinegar and happened to be painting on a certain day when they pulled in front of my house to go to somebody else's house. So, I walked out there, sat on the curb, and painted" on both cruisers.

The blue paint that he slapped on the vehicles stood out because they were white cars that featured a blue-and-gray accent stripe. His choice of what to paint on the doors of the cruisers left no doubt about the identity of the "artist." On one car, he painted his nickname, "Rusty," and on the side of the other vehicle, he drew the initial *R*.

Then he went back into his house. Minutes later, the officers returned to their cars and saw the personalized graffiti, which to them lacked any artistic merit. They didn't need hours of police academy training to figure out the identity of the culprit. When they went to the front door to confront the perp about the vandalism, he refused to come out. Instead, he gave them an obscene gesture through an open window and then tossed out an empty can of blue paint, which was the same blue paint that the cops saw on his right hand and on their cars.

"I stood in my door," he told the TV station. "I didn't want to come out because I knew what would happen." Yes, the cops would arrest him! "I threw an empty paint can out here, blue, the same color that I painted my name."

Police left but returned later and arrested him for criminal mischief. Sergeant Thomas Woodman told Bay News 9 that the graffiti didn't last long. The paint "was still wet at the time they found it," he said. "They immediately took it over to the paint and body shop and had it removed. The cost of doing so was approximately 140 dollars."

That was 10 dollars less than the 150-dollar bond the painter had to post before he was released from Pinellas County Jail.

When asked by Bay News 9 why he did it, the Gulfport man replied, "I was just being mischievous."

Honorable Mention: If you're driving and don't have a driver's license or car registration, you should try not to give the cops any reason to stop you. And yet a thirty-three-year-old woman, who had neither, drove around Perth, Australia, in 2016 in a white car with the word *POLICE* hand-drawn on it with a blue marker. Also marked on the sides of the car were blue and white checkered squares that crudely mimicked those displayed on the city's real police cruisers.

Understandably, the fake squad car—a Hyundai

that had no license plate—caught the attention of officers, who stopped the vehicle and tried to talk to the driver. At first, the woman locked the doors and refused to get out of the car. But eventually she did, and was cited for various traffic violations and ordered to appear in court. Her car was also impounded.

Luckily for the woman, her poor attempt to copy the police logo was not against the law because no one in their right mind would have mistaken her vehicle for a real squad car.

A witness took several pictures of the weird traffic stop and posted them on her Facebook page, spurring several comments. One person wrote, "I think we all just need to appreciate 'police' was spelled correctly." Another one said, "She'll probably go to court dressed as a judge."

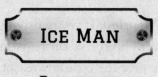

ICE MAN

BURGLARY

This bonehead could be the poster child for a criminal cold case. An ice-cold case, as in the frigid temperature of a freezer. Because that's where this burglary suspect was found hiding.

According to Miami-Dade police, early one

morning in 2013, the twenty-nine-year-old Miami man walked up to a Checkers Drive-In restaurant before it opened and shattered a window on the side of the building. When the morning crew, who were inside at the time, went to investigate, he yelled, "Give me everything!"

They gave him nothing. Instead, they all hustled to the other side of the restaurant and called police. He didn't take the hint that maybe he should split before the cops showed up. Instead, he picked up a concrete paver and hurled it through the closed drive-through window. Then he climbed through the opening. By now, all the employees had fled the restaurant, leaving him all alone.

Hearing the sirens of the squad cars, he chose not to make a run for it. He figured he would outsmart everyone by hiding in the restaurant—and what better place to hide than in the freezer? Never mind that it was below zero in there and he was wearing a short-sleeve shirt and shorts. He climbed inside the freezer and closed the lid. It brought him *cold comfort*.

When the employees went back inside the restaurant with the police, there was no sign of the intruder. Everyone assumed he had run off.

"About an hour into opening the restaurant, they hear some type of commotion inside," Miami-Dade police spokesman Sergeant Freddie Cruz told local TV station WFOR. "They see this gentleman come out of the freezer area." He obviously got *cold feet*. In fact, he was *chilled to the bone*. The shivering culprit staggered around because he had been inside the freezer with ice falling on him for more than an hour, said Cruz. Police responded quickly and arrested the cold-blooded suspect without further incident.

Emergency medical technicians were called to the scene to bandage the cuts he sustained in the freezer and from diving through the busted drive-through window. Bundled up in blankets, he was put into the backseat of a squad car and taken to jail, where he was booked on charges of burglary and criminal mischief. Hopefully, the arrest will have a *chilling effect* on any thoughts of future criminal activity.

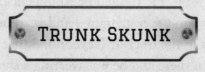

TRUNK SKUNK

CRIMINAL MISCHIEF

This blockhead faced a dilemma. He was trapped inside the trunk of a car and needed to call 911. But if he did, he knew he would get arrested. Why? Well, he unwittingly locked himself in the trunk after breaking into the vehicle.

According to Missoula (Montana) police, the thirty-one-year-old suspect was prowling in a neighborhood like a skunk late one night in 2015, looking for cars to break into. He thought he found a perfect target—a 2001 BMW parked outside Mountain Imports, an auto repair shop. Not wanting to bust any of the car's windows, which might alert residents in the immediate area, he quietly popped the trunk and climbed inside. He had planned to enter the interior of the car by crawling from the trunk through what he thought was a fold-down backseat.

The featherbrained thief hadn't counted on two things: One, the trunk automatically closed behind him and locked. Two, the backseat didn't fold down. Now he was stuck, a captive audience of one. He kicked and punched the backseat and the trunk. Nothing he tried could get him out of the predicament that he had brought on himself, so he remained trapped in the stuffy, pitch-black compartment.

Feeling a bit panicky, he knew he was out of options except for one—call 911. Of course, getting sprung from the trunk would also mean getting tossed in the slammer. But, hey, at this point, a brief stay in jail was better than remaining locked in the trunk for who knew how long.

The thief finally worked up his courage and made the call. Patrol Sergeant Colin Rose told radio station KGVO that 911 dispatch received a call from a man who said he had accidentally locked himself in the trunk of a car parked outside Mountain Imports. When police arrived, they contacted the owner of the business, who used a key to open the trunk and free the chump.

At first, the perp told responding officers that he had inadvertently fallen into the trunk. But the cops weren't falling for that ridiculous trunk bunk. "He was charged with all misdemeanors: criminal trespass to property, criminal trespass to a vehicle, and misdemeanor criminal mischief for damage he did to the car while trying to get out," Rose told the radio station. "This, in almost twenty-two years [of police work], was a brand-new occurrence."

☙ FOOLISH FUNSTERS ☙

ATTEMPTED THEFT

These two jokesters broke into a police van to take gag photos of themselves pretending they had been arrested. What was even funnier—although not to them—was that they accidentally locked themselves inside the vehicle and were arrested for real.

The pitiful pair, both in their early twenties, left a party at a condominium in the wee hours of the morning in 2011 in Radnor, Pennsylvania. They soon came upon an unattended police van in the parking lot. The state-owned vehicle, which served to transport prisoners, belonged to Radnor constable Mike Connor.

The two young men thought they were in luck when they discovered that the door in the back of the vehicle was not fully closed. According to police, the two dweebs climbed inside, closed the door, and began snapping pictures of each other pretending they were being hauled off to jail. They were having a great time until they tried to get out—and couldn't. They didn't know the van could only be unlocked from the outside as a security feature to keep prisoners from escaping.

Getting desperate, the captives tried to kick through the metal cage that separated the back interior of the van from the driver's compartment. That didn't work because the cage was designed to thwart prisoners. So the two idiots called a friend from the party. He showed up, but he couldn't open the door from the outside. Out of options, the friend called police at 3:57 a.m.

The cops soon phoned Officer Connor and woke him up. "I came down and unlocked the doors, and 'Dumb and Dumber' pranced out of the van," Connor told UPI. "They looked a little embarrassed. It was unbelievable."

The dorks no longer had to pretend they were riding to jail because they were arrested and put right back in the van for a trip to the local lockup. Among other charges, they were booked for attempted theft of a motor vehicle and criminal mischief.

On their way to jail, they had time to read Connor's collection of bumper stickers that he had plastered on the cage, such as WHOA. THIS IS LIKE A LIVE REALITY SHOW.

For the two pranksters, the joke was on them.

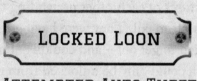

LOCKED LOON

ATTEMPTED AUTO THEFT

This bungling would-be thief wound up trapped in the car he was trying to steal because he ignorantly activated the automatic antitheft locking system. Adding to his woes, a crowd gathered to watch his unsuccessful effort to escape.

Car theft has been a huge problem in South Africa, with nearly eight hundred million dollars' worth of vehicles stolen in an *auto-graft* scheme. The figure would be much lower if the thieves were more like this hapless crook, who tried to steal Nosipho Mckay's BMW in Pretoria in 2014. Minutes after Mckay parked her car on a busy street and walked off to an appointment, the jughead used a special device to open the car, according to the *Star* newspaper.

The vehicle was smarter than he was because once he got inside and tried to start it, the car recognized that the driver was not the owner and automatically locked the doors, holding him captive. He pushed this button and that button and the handles of the other doors, but nothing worked. He was *under lock and key*. The more he tried to escape, the more panicky he became, which attracted onlookers and passersby.

Through the closed window, he told the crowd that he was accidentally trapped. He claimed he was one of the many "car guards" in the center of the city who kept an eye out for thieves. His tall tale was met with sarcastic laughter and insults by people who surrounded the vehicle and watched him flail around in the car for ninety agonizing minutes, the *Star* reported.

After police were called to the scene, they contacted Mckay, who showed up fifteen minutes later. According to the newspaper, "Mckay was stunned and in disbelief to find the suspect in her car. She yelled, 'What are you doing in my car?' before unlocking it. Officers from Pretoria Central Police Station promptly arrested him."

After he was put behind bars, he might have thought he *auto* not have done it.

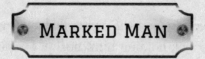

MARKED MAN

CRIMINAL MISCHIEF

This featherbrain wanted to leave his mark on history. Well, he did. But it's not the lasting legacy he wanted.

He used his car key to carve his name on the wall of the Alamo. On so many levels, this was a really stupid thing to do: 1. It's illegal to deface a historic monument. 2. His childish attempt at creating a mark for posterity cost tens of thousands of dollars to repair. 3. Of all the markings he could have notched, he etched his name, which told the world he was the culprit. 4. He did it in front of witnesses, who alerted authorities. 5. He ended up in jail.

The revered shrine of Texas liberty has stood for more than 250 years. During the Texas Revolution of 1836, frontiersman Davy Crockett and fellow defenders held out for thirteen days before an overwhelming force of Mexican troops killed them and captured the Alamo. However, Texas won its independence the following month, with soldiers rallying around the cry, "Remember the Alamo!"

The twenty-two-year-old carver from Laredo, Texas, and a female companion were among hundreds of tourists who visited the Alamo that day in 2015.

According to San Antonio police, he began carving his name into an interior limestone wall of an area of the Alamo chapel known as the Monks' Burial Room. Creating a three-inch-by-one-inch gash, he finished etching his first name in the wall. Before the culprit started carving his last name, a tour guide saw what he was doing and ordered him to stop. The perp and his companion then tried to flee out a back door, but an Alamo Ranger caught them, the *San Antonio Express-News* reported. The ranger handcuffed the goon and called police, who arrested him on charges of second-degree felony criminal mischief.

His name might have been engraved in stone, but it wasn't lasting. The room was closed off to visitors while preservation experts studied how to repair the costly damage, which was estimated at a whopping 250,000 dollars.

"Many Texans died here fighting for the independence of Texas," Alamo Rangers chief Mark Adkins told the media. "In Texas we take our history seriously and consider the Alamo to be sacred ground. Desecration [vandalism] of any part of these hallowed grounds, especially the walls of the Alamo Chapel, will not be tolerated."

It's likely this vandal will always remember the Alamo.

ABOUT THE AUTHOR

Allan Zullo is the author of more than one hundred nonfiction books on subjects ranging from sports and the supernatural to history and animals.

He has written the bestselling Haunted Kids series, published by Scholastic, which is filled with creepy stories based on, or inspired by, documented cases from the files of ghost hunters. He also has introduced Scholastic readers to the Ten True Tales series, about people who have met the challenges of dangerous, sometimes life-threatening, situations.

As a fan of the offbeat side of life, Allan is the author of such Scholastic books as *World's Dumbest Crooks and Other True Tales of Bloopers, Botches & Blunders*; *World's Dumbest Crooks 2*; *Fact or Fake? Test Your Smarts*; *Bad Pets*; *True Tales of Misbehaving Animals*; *Bad Pets Most Wanted!*; *Bad Pets on the Loose!*; and *Bad Pets Hall of Shame*.

Allan, the grandfather of five and the father of two grown daughters, lives with his wife, Kathryn, near Asheville, North Carolina. To learn more about the author, visit his website at www.allanzullo.com.